Latin American Monographs

Second Series

The Forgotten Ones

20

Center for Latin American Studies
University of Florida

The Forgotten Ones

Colombian Countrymen
in an
Urban Setting

Michael B. Whiteford

A University of Florida Book

The University Presses of Florida
Gainesville—1976

Latin American Monographs–Second Series

A University of Florida Book
sponsored by the
Center for Latin American Studies

Typography by Canon Graphics
Tallahassee, Florida

Printed by
STORTER PRINTING CO., INC.
Gainesville, Florida

Library of Congress Cataloging in Publication Data

Whiteford, Michael B   1945–
    The forgotten ones.

    (Latin American monographs; 2d ser., 20)
    "A University of Florida book."
    Bibliography: p.
    Includes index.
    1. Popayán, Colombia (City)—Poor.
    2. Popayán, Colombia (City)—Social conditions.
    3. Rural-urban migration—Colombia—Popayán (City)
    I. Title. II. Series: Florida. University,
Gainesville. Center for Latin American Studies.
Latin American monographs; 2d ser., 20.
HC198.P66W47   309.1′861′5   76-18066

ISBN 0-8130-0536-1

Dedicado con respecto y
admiración a: Aurelio, María,
Octavio, Jorge y Carmen, José y
María, Hernándo y Josefina, mi
ahijado Alirio, mis compadres
Luís y Mireya, Margot, y todos
los demás habitantes del
Barrio Tulcán.

Contents

Preface

THIS STUDY was something of a homecoming for me, as I had known Popayán since childhood, when my father, also an anthropologist, took us to live there in 1951–52 and again in 1962. Returning there in 1970 seemed quite a natural thing to do, and the prospect of seeing old acquaintances who would facilitate the transition into the field presented me with an advantage not shared by most of my colleagues on their initial major fieldwork expedition.

The first stage of fieldwork consisted of visiting the city's new areas and talking both with residents there and with people in town who knew about Popayán's recent growth. Originally, I had hoped to do a comparative study of two neighborhoods, a government-sponsored housing project and an independent development, but quickly realized that because of time constraints this would have to be postponed. At the same time I decided against studying a government housing project, for two reasons. First, a two-year residency requirement would eliminate recent arrivals to the city, people whose initial attitudes and reactions I wanted to study. Second, the stipulation that residents have a certain monthly income to qualify for the program would exclude many people in the low-income sector who do not have steady jobs as well as the very poor—segments of the population in which I was interested. (In the summer of 1974 I was able to spend three months in Popayán and began a study of a low-income government-sponsored housing project [cf. M. Whiteford 1976].)

Once I had decided to do a study of an independent development, choosing Barrio Tulcán was relatively simple, for my initial contacts with inhabitants were pleasant and the barrio's village-like appearance appealed to me at once.[1]

To Tulcaneses, my idea to study the barrio was not entirely novel. Before my arrival various groups—among them the Instituto de Crédito Territorial (Colombia's housing and urban development agency) and engineering and medical students from the local university—had undertaken short examinations of this, the city's poorest barrio. With the exception of an investigation by some medical students, who came weekly for one semester to visit specific families, these studies had lasted only a few days or weeks. What amazed residents was that my study and my interest in them lasted more than a couple of days, and this hastened and strengthened their confidence and trust in me. They were pleased and flattered that I wanted to do an in-depth study of them and was truly concerned with their views.

My methodological techniques differed little from those used by anthropologists doing more traditional rural studies (cf. M. Whiteford 1974a). Most of my information was collected during interviews which lasted from half an hour to two or three hours. Participant observation and watching the daily routine provided me with countless bits of useful information, and these exercises often served as good cross-checking devices. After I had been working in the barrio for four months and knew many of its inhabitants, I administered house-to-house census interviews. The camera proved to be useful, for once I let it be known that I would take pictures of families, I received a number of requests. This permitted me to meet people I otherwise might not have known, and returning a few days later with the print provided an opportunity for further contact. During the last month in Popayán, I administered and

1. The name of the barrio and its inhabitants are pseudonyms.

recorded a series of Thematic Apperception Tests. These techniques, plus the few existing documented materials on the barrio, provided the raw data for this study.

ACKNOWLEDGMENTS

My initial interest in anthropology must be credited to my father, Andrew H. Whiteford, who, by taking his family with him when he went into the field, provided me with an early and pleasant introduction to the discipline. Not only has he shared with me his data, his ideas, and the city in which he has worked since 1949, but he also has provided some valuable insights and suggestions regarding my own fieldwork. George M. Foster, my doctoral advisor and mentor at the University of California in Berkeley, first aroused my interest in changing peasant societies, which led to my study of migration. His comments and suggestions, both while I was in the field and during the writing of this book, have been invaluable. May N. Díaz and James F. King have also read this manuscript and I have benefited from their advice. I appreciated Robert V. Kemper's assistance in preparation of census data for the computer. Further, I want to thank Wayne Cornelius for suggesting the University Presses of Florida.

Colombian anthropologists Roberto Pineda Giraldo and Virginia Gutiérrez de Pineda provided useful and appreciated stimuli for me in the field. In Popayán, my work was enhanced by the cooperation of Luís Uribe Bravo, director of the Instituto de Crédito Territorial, who allowed me access to maps and other official documents of his organization. I am further indebted to Víctor Caicedo Arboleda and Tulia Elvira Angulo de Velasco for their valuable insights on change in Popayán. The fieldwork on which this research is based was supported by the National Institutes of Health (National Institute of General Medical Sciences), Training Grant GM-1224, and financial assistance from the Center for Latin American Studies, University of California, Berkeley. I also acknowledge with gratitude the support from the Wenner-Gren Foundation for Anthropological Research in providing funds for the 1974 follow-up study on which chapter 10 is based.

Parts of this book have appeared elsewhere. Chapter 2 was first published in an altered and expanded form as "Barrio Tulcán: Fieldwork in a Colombian City," in G. M. Foster and

R. V. Kemper, eds., *Anthropologists in Cities* (Boston: Little, Brown, and Co., 1974). Chapters 3 and 5 were originally published as "Neighbors at a Distance: Social Relations in a Low-Income Colombian Barrio," in W. A. Cornelius and F. M. Trueblood, eds., *Latin American Urban Research*, vol. 4, *Anthropological Perspectives on Latin American Urbanization* (Beverly Hills, Calif.: Sage Publications, 1974).

My greatest debt is to the people of Barrio Tulcán for providing me with an invaluable experience and with many pleasant memories. I regret not being able to acknowledge them fully, but an overriding concern with respecting their privacy and protecting the confidentiality of their lives prevents me from doing this. When, in 1974, I told a number of them I was writing a book about Tulcán, they regarded it as an honor. The honor is mine, and I hope this book provides an adequate vehicle for the expression of their thoughts and views. To my wife, Patty, I owe special thanks; her unfailing interest in my work and her perceptive insights and suggestions were important to the eventual success of the project. She provided an important and immeasurable element of encouragement both during the period of fieldwork and while writing the book.

1. "All the world is Popayán"

ANTHROPOLOGY, which for so long concentrated on the study of isolated hunters and gatherers, tribal peoples, and peasant societies, in recent years has experienced what is literally an explosion in the number of anthropological investigations which deal with aspects of city life and urban society. While at first glance this shift in focus may appear new to anthropology, the work of W. Lloyd Warner and his colleagues and students throughout the 1940s and 1950s (e.g., Warner and Lunt 1941, 1942; Warner and Srole 1945; Warner et al. 1949; Davis, Gardner, and Gardner 1941) and the research of the British anthropologists in Africa (e.g., Banton 1957; A. L. Epstein 1957, 1958, 1967; Gutkind 1960, 1961; Mayer 1961, 1962; Mitchell 1951, 1956, 1960, 1966) have shown that such a shift, in fact, is neither new nor novel to the discipline. Nevertheless, what we are now witnessing is a new and sizable change of emphasis, with more anthropologists doing urban work than ever before, with a greater number of anthropology course offerings dealing with urban phenomena, with new books on the subject (cf. Foster and Kemper, eds. 1974; Southall, ed. 1973; Friedl and Chrisman, eds. 1975; Weaver and White, eds. 1972; Cornelius and Trueblood, eds. 1974; Uzzell and Provencher 1976), and

1

with even an anthropological journal devoted exclusively to the study of urban society. These changes in quantity and scope represent a new commitment to the urban aspects of human existence.

Among anthropologists interested in Latin America, this new shift in the direction of urban fieldwork really began with Oscar Lewis' pioneering work (1952) on the effects of rural-urban migration among Tepoztecans living in Mexico City. As a result of Lewis' study, three models for urban anthropologists seemed to emerge. First, for many scholars, urban anthropology has been equated with the problem of why and how people become urbanized, particularly in the movement of rural peoples to cities. This concern with rural migrants may be explained in part by anthropologists' traditional rural bias; consequently, many urban studies have been the products of anthropologists who worked in the countryside and who packed up and followed their subjects to the city. Second, as Lewis did in his early work, a number of anthropological investigators have dealt with urban dwellers who migrated from specific rural areas (e.g., Butterworth 1962; Lewis 1952; Orellana 1973; Kemper 1971, 1974). A third common aspect of many urban anthropological studies derived from Lewis has been the focus on low-income neighborhoods (e.g., Peattie 1968; Mangin 1967a, 1967b; Safa 1974; Lewis 1959; Roberts 1970, 1973). In part this is a reflection of the fact that poor neighborhoods are the loci where rural migrants tend to live; the emphasis on the neighborhood can be attributed to most anthropologists' personal tastes and methodological orientations. In the neighborhood, like the village, the anthropologist in the course of a year or so can get to know most, if not all, of the community's inhabitants. This personalistic aspect of fieldwork so important to anthropology—seeing and interacting daily with the same, relatively small group of people—is too often lost in the city. As Andrew Whiteford notes: "Such approaches as sampling techniques, the use of census data, and statistical analysis of masses of data would appear to be absolutely necessary for understanding [cities], but their use also tends to impersonalize the research and deprive the worker of his most satisfying experience, the personal identification with the people being studied" (1960:2).

Thus, in the past fifteen to twenty years a growing body of

urban anthropological literature has evolved. However, most of these studies occurred in the large, industrialized, often capital cities of Latin America. The effect is that many statements and generalizations about the nature of urban life, even among the urban poor, tend to be based on information from places like Bogotá, Mexico City, Lima, and Buenos Aires. Obviously, the importance of these cities cannot be ignored, but numerically they constitute only a fraction of the total number of Latin American urban areas. For example, in discussing "city life" in Mexico, Jack Rollwagen points out that the majority of studies are on Mexico City itself, followed by investigations of Guadalajara and Monterrey (1972:70). Yet, these cities "comprise only 3/256th of all cities in Mexico and their combined populations total 1/3 (33.63 per cent) of the total number of the inhabitants of cities in Mexico" (Rollwagen 1972:70).

Data for the smaller, provincial, intermediate cities are not so abundant (e.g., A. Whiteford 1960; Price 1973; Epstein 1972; Hammel 1969; González 1974; Reina 1973; Pi-Sunyer 1973). These cities are often regional capitals, the exception being Epstein's work on Brasilia, with little or no industry and populations ranging from 10,000–20,000 to 200,000. Clearly, knowledge about these secondary cities is important to the conceptual and theoretical framework of urban studies and the processes of urbanization. These studies are of a different tradition and do not derive from Lewis' model. They are investigations of cities *sui generis* and are done by anthropologists who are doing with cities, albeit relatively small ones, what their colleagues have done with villages.

Popayán, the city in which the following study was conducted, is one such intermediate-sized city. With an estimated population of 77,000 in 1970 (DNP 1969:57), Popayán's population reflects a considerable increase from the 31,866 and 58,500 inhabitants recorded in the 1951 and 1963 censuses. One natural result of this population increase is an expanding city periphery with new barrios. In Popayán's case, this growth has been rather orderly, and its outskirts do not have the half-grown appearance and the disorderly urban sprawl characteristic of many other Latin American cities. While some of these new neighborhoods are being built by private contractors for Popayán's upper and middle classes, who gradually are moving out from the city's center, most of the construction is being done by the Colombian government's housing and urban development agency, the Instituto de Crédito Territorial (ICT), to accommodate the influx of rural migrants.

This volume represents the results of a year-long investigation of one of these new neighborhoods—Tulcán, a barrio of 1,780 inhabitants located on the edge of Popayán. Its objectives are fourfold. First, it is basically a community study, a holistic analysis of a particular barrio. As such, it contains materials pertaining to a variety of aspects of Tulcanés life. Second, because 80 per cent of the barrio's household heads were born outside of Popayán, and since most of these families migrated to Popayán within the past fifteen years, throughout the book there is an underlying concern with migration. Third, residents of Tulcán are poor people, both by their own standards as well as by those of the larger community. They are not poor in a spiritual sense and are not without joie de vivre, but they are deprived in a social, economic, and political sense. This book attempts to portray their poverty and way of life as they might describe it; this attempt is the most important aspect of the study, as the poor generally are not well understood. Its contribution to the small but expanding body of knowledge about poor people will perhaps contribute to the alleviation of their desperate condition. Finally, as mentioned above, the setting is in an intermediate-sized city and —although this report is not about the total city of Popayán (cf. A. Whiteford 1960, 1976)—information about low-income peoples and how they regard their surroundings is essential for a better understanding of secondary cities and for the comprehension of the urbanization process in general.

POPAYÁN

In December 1536, a group of Spanish soldiers under the command of Sebastián de Belalcázar set up camp in the Pubenza Valley next to a small group of Indians. Earlier that year, Belalcázar, a lieutenant in the forces of Francisco Pizarro, had left Quito to search for the illusive and legendary El Dorado (Castrillon 1970:3). Now, months later, he made camp and founded a city at the foot of a hill, where today a statue in his likeness watches over Popayán.[1]

1. There is some disagreement over the spelling of the founder's name. Both Belalcázar and Benalcázar appear in the literature. Payanés historian

Located slightly more than two degrees above the equator, but at an altitude of 5,773 feet and with a temperature which averages in the mid-sixties (Fahrenheit), the Pubenza Valley is free of many lowland tropical diseases; it was therefore a natural site for establishing a regional capital, later to become the seat of the Department of Cauca. Within a few years after its founding, Popayán was a city of considerable importance. Ten years after its establishment, Pope Paul III made it an episcopal see, and in "1558 the Crown granted it an escutcheon and the title 'very noble and very loyal city'" (Crist 1950:131). Popayán's role as a city of eminence and power continued to grow, and by the middle of the seventeenth century, it governed 670,000 square kilometers, more than half of the 1,272,813 square kilometers which comprise present-day Colombia (Castrillon 1970:6). For a number of years, Popayán was matched only by Bogotá in authority and prestige in northern South America.

The role of Popayán's elite in Colombia's history is significant. "Sixteen presidents of Colombia came from Popayán; its families produced numerous archbishops, ambassadors and other diplomats, and generals—sometimes for both sides—in the civil wars of the 19th century" (A. Whiteford 1960:6). Today one is continually reminded of Popayán's past glories and greatness by the marble plaques on the facades of buildings which note the birthplaces of great leaders in Colombia's history—Tomás Cipriano de Mosquera, Camilo Torres, José Caldas, José Hilario López, Guillermo Valencia—and point out the houses where other historical figures, such as Antonio José de Sucre, Simón Bolívar, and Alexander von Humboldt, stayed.

Popayán retained much of its power and importance until the middle of the nineteenth century, when wars and the

---

Arcesio Aragón prefers the former, stating that its spelling appears in the chronicles started by the conquistador and is the appellation used by his son (1930:8). There is also dissent regarding the date assigned to the founding of the city. Historians conclude it took place between 1536 and 1538, although they vary on the exact time (Martínez 1959:20–21). Finally, there is some discrepancy pertaining to the origin of the name Popayán. Martínez agrees with those who suggest it is a corruption of the Quechua *pampayan*, composed of *pampa* and *yan*, meaning "place where the river passes" and referring to the Cauca River (1959:31). Aragón suggests Popayán could have come from a combination of the indigenous words *Puben-Yasguen* or perhaps was the name of a sovereign who ruled there at the time of the conquest (1930:23–24).

ensuing departure to Pasto, Cali, and Bogotá of some of its rich and able families changed the situation. At the same time, new departments were carved out of Cauca, taking over many of Popayán's mineral and productive agricultural regions. Divested of its former territory and isolated from the rest of the country by the cordilleras, Popayán had by 1905 an area of only 30,727 square kilometers (Castrillon 1970:15).

As Popayán's national role diminished, the city, with geographical assistance, isolated itself. It was not until 1926 that Popayán was connected by railroad to Cali, an industrial center just 150 kilometers to the north, and to the Pacific port of Buenaventura. Highway connections with Pasto, to the south, were not established until the 1930s and then only because of an impending war with Peru, and Cali was not reached by a hard-surface road until 1962. As late as the 1950s, Popayán's influential families were able to prevent any industry from taking hold. Popayán was content to supply Colombia with poets, presidents, and religious leaders while at the same time shutting itself off from encroachments from the outside world. Although change is now occurring, the attitudes of many of its residents remain much the same, because, as Payaneses are fond of saying, "All the world is Popayán."

TULCÁN

The barrio of Tulcán is located in the southwest corner of Popayán, half an hour's walk from the city's central Parque de Caldas. Geographically it stands apart from the city; a distance of no less than a kilometer separates the houses of the barrio from those of its nearest neighbor, Barrio Alfonso López. The barrio is hidden by a tall, thick barrier of willows, bamboo, eucalyptus, and cypress trees, a field occupied by the decaying kiln of a brick factory, the women's prison compound, and the concrete cattle-pens of the municipal stockyards. The entrance to the barrio is a well-traveled dirt road which skirts along the perimeter of the stockyards. Tulcán is situated at the juncture of two small streams, the Río Guadua and the Quebrada de las Dos Agüitas, above which rise grassy hills speckled with grazing cattle.

To the casual observer, Tulcán appears more rural than urban. Chickens, ducks, sleeping dogs, and an occasional pig or horse vie for space in its narrow dirt streets with bicyclists,

FIGURE 1. Panorama of Barrio Tulcán.

men pushing two-wheeled carts, women balancing heavy shopping baskets on their heads, and periodic cattle drives through the barrio. Large plots of *yuca* (sweet manioc), corn, coffee, and bananas, as well as a variety of other garden vegetables, add to the country ambience, while the hodgepodge of architectural styles further sets the barrio apart from colonial Popayán. Even the bright yellows and greens of the painted houses distinguish the barrio from the more subdued hues and tones of the town. When inhabitants say they are "going to Popayán," they acknowledge more than the obvious spatial separation between town and barrio.

BARRIO HISTORY

Tulcán is a relatively new barrio. It is also a poor barrio. Unlike most products of the city's present expansion programs, it was not built by the ICT. Until seven years ago, the area which now constitutes the Barrio Tulcán was used for digging clay for one of the many small brick factories in the area. At that time, it was known only as *las dos agüitas*, a reference to the two streams, and there was only a sprinkling of houses along the road which twisted through the tract en route to the hilltop house of a Payanés farmer. In 1964, Juan Acevedo, owner of the clay pit since 1953, decided to abandon the unprofitable brick-making business. Distressed by the poor living conditions of many of his employees, he tried to get the Instituto to buy the land for low-cost housing. When they showed no interest, he subdivided the land himself, parceling the area into 164 lots of various shapes and sizes, ranging in prices from about 25 cents to 75 cents (U.S.) per square meter. (At the time of the study, the exchange rate was approximately 19.50 Colombian pesos to the U.S. dollar. In this book, unless otherwise indicated, the $ sign indicates pesos, as is the custom in Colombia.) The price depended on the quality of the lot, which in turn was based on how much of the property was "solid ground" and how much consisted of holes left over from the clay-mining operations. Roads were laid out, the beginnings of a sewer network were installed, and Acevedo loaned an electric transformer to the new barrio. In addition, he donated land to be used for a school, a chapel, a health center, and the barrio assembly hall. His goal to provide inexpensive land and easy terms of purchase for the poor was soon realized, for within a year he had sold all of the land.

DEMOGRAPHIC OVERVIEW

Once, while watching a group of shouting children chase each other through the streets of Tulcán, a resident dryly remarked that the world was being overrun by the young. Judging only by her immediate surroundings, it is easy to understand her remark. Tulcán is a barrio of the young: the average age is nineteen years, with a median age of fourteen.[2] More important, 54 per cent of the barrio's population is fifteen years old or younger, with 29 per cent being under the age of ten. There are very few senior citizens; less than 1 per cent (N=14) of the residents are sixty-five years old or older. Of the total barrio population, 51 per cent (N=895) were born outside of Popayán, but of those who are sixteen and over, the percentage of migrants jumps to 75 per cent. Women (N=928) outnumber men (N=852), with proportionately more of them (51 per cent to 48 per cent) being born outside Popayán. However, of those 15 and over, 72 per cent of the males are migrants as compared to 52 per cent of the women. In short, Tulcán is a barrio of migrants and, like Colombia as a whole, has a young population (DANE 1967:29).

THE DAILY ROUND

For most of the barrio's inhabitants, the daily round varies little. The barrio comes to life shortly after sunrise and settles down at dusk, a natural occurrence in an area where the majority of dwellings are without electric light. For most families,

2. Data here are based on my complete house-to-house census-interviews of the barrio. During the count of the barrio, the unit of analysis was the household, which emically was defined as consisting of those people who live under the same roof, share living quarters, and cook and eat together, regardless of whether they are related. In numerous cases, two or more families shared a house and had joint living and sleeping quarters, and although they used the same kitchen facilities, they cooked and ate their meals separately. They were counted as separate households. The naming of the household head was left up to the members of the household and was based on a number of possible criteria, such as who was oldest, chief breadwinner, and the like. People were specific and unwavering in their choices. Even when two unrelated families were living together as one household, everyone knew who the household head was.

the morning begins with a cup of hot chocolate or coffee and a couple of hard rolls. The men then set off for work, the children get ready for school, and the women leave for Popayán to do their daily shopping. For the women of Tulcán, the trip to town is a pleasant break, one of the few opportunities they have to leave the house. When they return between nine-thirty and ten to begin preparing the main meal of the day, there is very little going on in the barrio. The tranquillity of the morning is interrupted only by a crying baby, the occasional raucous noise of a taxi's horn, and the sounds of the ubiquitous radio soap operas.

As the morning progresses, more people appear in the streets. Adolfo Gonzáles sets up his vegetable stand at the barrio's entrance and a continuous, changing group of women begin buying—usually a peso's worth of bananas, or a few pieces of yuca for the day's *sancocho* (a Caucano stew). David Narváez or Victor Muñoz will make a few trips back to the barrio in his horse-drawn cart, always with a group of boys chasing behind wanting a ride. Impromptu soccer games materialize on the barrio's main streets, and there is almost always a cadre of eight-to-ten-year-olds playing marbles next to Angelina Ordóñez's house.

From eleven-thirty until one o'clock in the afternoon, there is a continuous trickle of women and children on the road leading out of the barrio, carrying the *comida*, the main meal of the day, to the working members of the family. This meal usually consists of cooked yuca or potatoes, bread, a beef or chicken stew, and a bowl of rice. At the same time, school children, along with men who are able to return, hasten back, the latter stopping for a moment to chat with a neighbor, to buy a couple of cigarettes in a housefront store, or to remind a son not to linger too long fishing for guppies in the Río Guadua.

The afternoon finds the barrio more active. The number of soccer games in the streets and vacant lots increases, and men who work nights in the stockyards or mornings selling produce in the market now visit or sit on a curb playing cards or a variation of Chinese checkers. By late afternoon, the women finish their work and come outside. Between five and six, the streets begin to fill with people relaxing from the day's work, and only when the late afternoon shadows creep down the hillsides do families return to their houses for supper of bread rolls and a cup of coffee. An occasional shout is heard in Micaela de Miranda's cantina, and the volume of a particular radio may be turned up for a favorite *cumbia*, but these noises quickly cease, and by eight or nine o'clock the barrio shuts down for the night.

On Saturday afternoons, Sundays, and holidays, the barrio always seems crowded. People from other poor barrios in town like to stroll out to Tulcán, and couples daydream arm-in-arm as they follow their favorite soccer team or listen to the trials and tribulations of Colombia's current radio and television heroine in "Simplemente María" on their transistor radios. Many stop at Eva de Angulo's stand at the entrance to the barrio to buy warm beer, pop, hot *arepas* (Colombian tortillas), or pig cracklings. Families, their lunches in cane baskets and their bottles of *aguardiente* (an anise-flavored liquor) under their arms, walk through the barrio on their way to a picnic area along the Río Guadua on the far side of the settlement. *Bambuco* music played at ear-shattering decibels readily identifies the barrio cantinas, where the occupants sit quietly sipping their drinks. Jaime Arroyo's *tejo* courts always have a crowd. Tejo, a Colombian game similar to quoits, is played at one end of a lot and at the other end men compete at *sapo*, another Colombian game, to determine who pays for the next round of drinks. Outside the tejo courts, Jaime's wife, María Eugenia, and mother-in-law, Diosolina de Gutiérrez, prepare tamales and empanadas as they gossip and chat amiably with passersby.

These are times for visiting, and *solares* (house yards which may include a garden) serve as informal meeting grounds for families and friends. On these days, Tulcaneses flock to the cockfights or the movies, and the nearby Teatro Bolívar, the theater of the "popular class," always is assured of a good crowd when it presents a double feature of Mexican cowboy movies.

THE LITTLE COMMUNITY

Tulcaneses have group consciousness—although they lack cohesion—and, with few exceptions, possess a great deal of pride in their barrio. Former president of the Pro-Barrio Junta de Acción Comunal (the barrio's elected governing council),

Miguel Agredo, once gave me an hour's lecture on why Tulcán is so different and so much better than the other new barrios around Popayán. He attributed this to the lengthy struggle the barrio went through in order to get electricity and municipal water service. Miguel contends this fight made the people conscious that they are part of Tulcán and that they have an investment in the barrio. People enjoyed telling me that Tulcán was the poorest barrio in the city and then explaining why it was the best. They always mentioned the barrio's school, health center, and municipal services, but most importantly, they stressed that its citizens were not "crude and vulgar."

At one Junta meeting, Adolfo Samboni stood up and spoke for ten minutes on barrio responsibility. He began his speech by telling the assembly that Tulcán was the best of the poor barrios, citing the above reasons. Then he cautioned them to think of the barrio before doing things which might reflect badly on Tulcán. He reminded them to be careful when selling or renting their houses, so that future Tulcaneses would be people of good character, and further instructed them to use "good manners and intelligence" in the city, explaining that Tulcán did not want to acquire a reputation like that of its neighbor Barrio Alfonso López, regarded by Tulcaneses as an area of thugs, drunkards, and vagabonds. There were general murmurs of agreement. Another time, Luís Santa Cruz told me, "You can leave your door open here when you go out and nothing will happen. In Popayán if you leave your door open and look the other way, you will lose your radio and everything else." Whenever a robbery occurs in the barrio or a fight takes place in a cantina, the troublemakers are branded as outsiders from Barrio Alfonso López. Faustina de Arias described Tulcaneses as "honorable people." Somehow, despite its poverty, Tulcán always emerges with a favorable glow when its residents compare it to other barrios in the city. (Barrio chauvinism is not characteristic only of Tulcán. People in other sections of town seem to have similar perceptions of their areas vis-à-vis Tulcán, Pandiguando, Esmeralda, and other low-income neighborhoods. Residents of Barrio Alfonso López, for example, feel that their barrio, particularly when they compare it to Tulcán, is a much safer and more respectable place to live.)

ON THE FRINGE

It would not be correct to exclude Tulcán from Popayán, and yet it is not an integral part of the city. Tulcaneses are "marginal" to Popayán. Geographically the barrio is separated from the city; socially and economically the distance is perhaps greater. Socially, they are, by their own definition as well as that of outsiders, members of the lower class. Their participation in most Payanés activities is minimal. Their role is one of an audience rather than of actors. Economically they are concerned with the essentials of making ends meet from one day to the next. Politically, while not disenfranchised, they have no power and no voice in nominating or appointing local officials. They feel, with good reason, that they are the forgotten ones.

2. Leaving the Countryside

Migration to the City

B ECAUSE four-fifths of its household heads come from outside
Popayán, Tulcán can be classified as a barrio of migrants.
The presence of migrants in the cities often is attributed to an
amorphous, slightly ambiguous "push-pull" syndrome (cf. Herrick 1965:13–15; Kemper 1970:8; Matos Mar 1961:182–90;
Germani 1961:212–14). Although it has heuristic value, this
model is too simplistic to explain the many subtleties involved
in the reasons why country people move to urban areas. People move to the cities not for any single reason, but rather
because of a combination of factors. Among these are economic
incentives, desire to educate children, need for medical care,
and the fascination of the city (cf. M. Whiteford 1976).

CAUSES FOR MOVEMENT

Economic incentives combined with land pressures are the
most common reasons for migrating. The vast majority of
Tulcanés migrants were peasant farmers before leaving for the
city, having cultivated a number of crops on their small farms
which, along with their supply of animals, kept them relatively

14

self-sufficient. The major portion of what they raised was used for internal consumption, with their cash income coming from the sale of surplus vegetables in the local markets or of coffee and *cabuya* (sisal or hemp), which were sold in the cities or to larger farmers. Traditionally, they were able to get along quite well this way.

Population increases, primarily due to a drop in infant mortality in recent years, and an inefficient traditional agricultural technology work together to create land shortages, forcing migration (Camacho de Pinto 1970:62). For the southern Colombian peasant, land shortages have been coupled with a decline in coffee prices in recent years, creating an even more difficult situation. Many Tulcaneses who come to Popayán searching for employment feel as though they literally were pushed off their land. Like numerous other small peasant farmers, they eventually decide they have no viable alternative except to abandon the countryside and turn toward the urban centers for solutions to their economic problems.

At the same time, other Colombian peasants are attracted to the city. Their economic situation in the countryside is not desperate, and they move to the city more because they see it as an opportunity for a better life than because such a move is the only possible solution to a problem. This latter group generally consists of young men and women without families, who have less at stake than those who were pushed off the land. In the city they hope to find high-paying jobs which will bring them closer to obtaining the "good life."

Another reason for moving to the city is the migrants' expressed desire to educate their children. As in many countries, Colombia's rural schools are not as good as its urban ones, even at the primary level, and most secondary schools are concentrated in the large cities. Furthermore, rural schools frequently are located long distances from where families live, and children often are needed at home to work the land, creating additional difficulties in acquiring an education. Thus, the peasant must leave the countryside if he wishes to educate his children thoroughly.

Among Tulcaneses, education is regarded as an important factor in obtaining a better life. Some individuals are able to combine the desires of educating children and maintaining life in the country. They keep their farms, but move the family into town while the husband alternates his time between city and country. Marco Astaiza, who specifically came to Tulcán to educate his two youngest children, spends one week every month with his family in the barrio; the other three weeks of the month he tends his farm with his eldest son and other relatives who have remained in the country. Other families admit to having suffered financial losses when they left their farms in order to educate their offspring.

Health reasons also are cited for moving to the city, for the paucity of medical facilities in the countryside necessitates migration to obtain any type of intensive or prolonged treatment. Some have migrated to Popayán because they feel it has a "healthier" climate than that of their previous home. Popayán is not as cold and rainy as are some of the highland areas in the region nor is it as hot and humid as much of the nearby Department of Valle.

In a few instances, an expressed desire to break away from the confines of the peasant community is the catalyst for movement. Some individuals feel they have to leave their place of origin if they ever are going to improve their lives. Speaking on this subject, Manuel Calderón says, "In a man's own land he's nobody." He theorizes that in order to improve socially as well as economically, "you have to move to neutral territory. In one's own place of birth, people have to keep their neighbors at their level. If you try to progress, they feel threatened and will try to prevent it through slander, gossip, and perhaps going so far as killing the individual rather than letting him improve his situation." Referring to his former neighbors, Pedro Angulo notes, "They want to see you at their level, or, better said, at a level worse than theirs."

People move for various other reasons. A few women, like Eva de Angulo and Lucilia de Granada, were brought to Popayán as teenage girls to work as servants for Payanés families. Paco Díaz was discharged from the Colombian army while stationed in Popayán, and since the city appealed to him, he remained. Other individuals migrate to be with members of their family already there. Samuel Paz, who left a well-paying job in a sugarcane plantation near Cali to move in with his parents when they moved to Tulcán, says, "One has an obligation to come back and live with the old ones." Hoping to avoid the wrath of vengeful relatives, Hernán Granada moved to Popayán after getting into a machete fight with a drinking partner.

Although Colombia's two decades of internal strife have been cited in the literature as factors creating considerable internal migration (cf. Guzmán Campos et al. 1962:295–96; Pineda 1960; Lipman and Havens 1965:244; Flinn 1966:8–9), only a few Tulcaneses suggested it as a cause for movement. In fact, in most cases migrants came from areas not badly affected by the violence.[1]

RESULTS OF MOVEMENT

It is not difficult to ascertain to what extent the migrants' goals have been realized. Those who came to Popayán for non-economic reasons generally have been successful in their endeavors. For those who moved for economic reasons, the results may not seem so clear. Once a migrant arrives in Popayán, he is faced with the prospect of finding some form of employment, and the dreams of obtaining well-paying jobs are realized by only a few. The best jobs are with Popayán's two industries—the liquor-bottling plant and Empaques del Cauca, manufacturers of hemp sacks—and with either municipal or departmental governments. Yet, collectively, they provide only a few jobs, employing only about a tenth of the Tulcanés household-head labor force. Less desirable forms of employment are also difficult to obtain. Consequently, Tulcanés migrants find themselves counting on their own ingenuity to support themselves and their families in ways that are not particularly lucrative. Nevertheless, urban life still seems attractive. Few Tulcaneses indicate any desire to move back to their place of birth. While some of them occasionally speak of nostalgia for certain aspects of country life, most insist that no circumstances would induce them to leave the city.

POPAYÁN AS A CHOICE

It is surprising that individuals choose to migrate to Popayán, a city with very little industry and hence little to offer in the way of employment. Cali, a city of a million inhabitants, sec-

1. McGreevey writes that rural violence, although often mentioned as one of the principal causes for rural-urban migrafion, with few exceptions has

ond largest and one of the most industrial cities in Colombia, is located only 150 kilometers from Popayán and would seem to be a more natural choice. Yet there are a number of plausible explanations as to why Popayán is selected instead, which may throw some light on the general processes and problems of migration in Colombia.

Many of Tulcán's inhabitants either are natives of the area just south of Popayán or lived there just prior to coming to the city. For them proximity is the key: Popayán is closer than Cali, and as such is the first city available to the migrants when they leave the countryside.

Some individuals spend a couple of years in Popayán and then move on to Cali or other larger cities. For them Popayán may serve as the first stage in the process of "step migration" to larger, more industrialized cities. With Cali only two hours away by bus, however, proximity to Popayán as a reason for its choice may seem unconvincing as the determining factor in this process. Nevertheless, for poor rural families, any uprooting and movement is a financial hardship of considerable proportions. Popayán therefore may be seen as a place where they can add to their resources before continuing the journey. Some people come to Popayán intending to stay only a short time, but end up as more or less permanent residents. For example, Miguel López intended Popayán to be only a step to the Department of Huila when he and his family of six left Bolívar, Cauca, in 1965. When they arrived in Popayán, they moved in with relatives, while Miguel and his son looked for work which would finance their bus fares to the city of Neiva. One thing led to another, and the departure was continually postponed. Now the López family is firmly settled in Tulcán, and the possibility of going to Huila seems remote.

Another explanation for settling in Popayán is that many have friends or relatives already living there. They hear about life in Popayán from a cousin or a former neighbor when he returns to the *vereda* (a small political subdivision). Then, when they decide to move to the city, they choose Popayán because they have an idea of what to expect, and know someone who can help them find housing and a job. Often people

not played a significant role in total interdepartmental movement of people (1968:213–14). Cardona's study of two squatter settlements in Bogotá supplies similar data (1968:63).

stay with friends from their natal villages while they scout out employment possibilities. Then, if they decide to stay, they board a bus and return home for their families. After Osvaldo and Elsa Castellanos moved to Tulcán, a stream of visiting relatives stayed with them for varying periods while they tested the winds, trying to decide whether they too wanted to make the move.

For most people, the decision to go to Popayán instead of another urban area is a direct and conscious one. Most adult Tulcaneses, at one time or another, have been to Cali, either as visitors or residents; in fact, 78 per cent (N=213) of all present barrio household heads have previously been there, while a surprising 26 per cent (N=72) have made the twenty-hour bus ride to Bogotá. Migrant-nonmigrant differences are minor: of the former, 76 per cent (N=166) have been to Cali and 26 per cent (N=57) have visited Bogotá, and of the latter, 83 per cent (N=47) have gone to Cali and 26 per cent (N=15) have been as far as Bogotá. In short, a majority of Tulcaneses know something of Colombia's large cities, so it may be assumed that their presence in Popayán is more planned than accidental.

Another explanation for choosing Popayán reflects one of Colombia's most serious and pressing socioeconomic problems: unemployment. A number of Tulcaneses have lived in Cali and Bogotá but, finding no work there, have come to Popayán. These people express the peculiar truism that it is less costly to be un- or underemployed in Popayán than in Bogotá or Cali. Those who have lived in either of these large cities also say that they prefer Popayán because it is a safe, quiet city, without most of the problems of crime they experienced in the larger cities. Thus, many Tulcaneses present a new twist on the standard theories of migration, in which the individual ends up living in the large industrial centers. Data from Tulcán indicate that some people go to the large city and then, for one reason or another, reject it and seek a smaller and economically less attractive city in which to live.

Tulcaneses also have experimented with living in other small communities, in addition to having resided in larger cities, before eventually settling in Popayán. Adolfo and María Gonzáles gave up trying to farm in Bolívar, Cauca, and moved to Morales, Cauca, where Adolfo taught school and continued to farm. From there they went to Popayán for medical reasons. Primitivo Obregón changed from agricultural work in the highlands to farming in the tropical lowland before migrating to Popayán. In all, the average Tulcanés migrant family has moved 2.3 times before coming to Popayán.

Many Tulcaneses are "return-migrants" (cf. Feindt and Browning 1970), i.e., they have moved from the country to Popayán, then on to another city or back to the country, before eventually returning to Popayán. Twenty-six per cent of migrant household heads previously had lived in Popayán and then moved away. These people are not seasonal migrants, but simply are trying to find a better life. Most have never really been satisfied with what they have found. Jorge Cruz is a good example of the return-migrant. Jorge left his native village as a young man "to get to know other parts of the country." He worked in Pereira, Cauca, on a coffee plantation for a couple of years and then spent time in Costa Rica, Valle, as a peasant farmer on an uncle's farm and in Santa Leticia Moscopán, Huila, as a lumberjack, before moving to Popayán in 1955. In Popayán, Jorge worked in construction for two years, married a migrant woman from Puracé, Cauca, and had two children. Later, he and a friend went to Cali and obtained work on a road construction crew, but before the year was up, Jorge decided to return to his place of birth to try his hand at farming again. After a year on his family's farm, it was clear to him that he could not support his family (which by then included four children) there; so they moved back to Popayán. Perhaps frequent moves indicate that the return-migrant is more actively seeking a better life than are other migrants.

There are also people who stay in Popayán but would prefer to move elsewhere. Many would like to return to the country and resume their previous ways of life, but they remember leaving the countryside in the first place because they were unable to make an adequate living tilling the soil. So they stay, discontented with their present situation but unsure how they can remedy it. Only a few eventually do return to the country.

Most Tulcaneses, migrants and native-born alike, regard their move to the barrio as a semipermanent one. Among migrants, 66 per cent (N=145) are homeowners, while the Payanés-born show an equally high percentage (65 per cent

[N=37]) of proprietors. Their intention of permanence is reflected in their manner of occupancy.

Although Tulcanés migration is a complex phenomenon which varies with each individual case, four general patterns of movement emerge. In the first, the migrant goes from one rural place to another. In the second, he combines movement in the rural hinterlands with forays of varying duration to urban centers. In the third, the migrant is characterized only by inter- and intra-urban movement, having given up on the countryside as a viable alternative. The fourth pattern, which includes aspects of the others, is return-migration.

There is a feeling among the migrant population that their situation is a definite improvement over what it was before coming to Popayán. But in some ways, they feel they are just as far from obtaining the "good life" as they were in the country because their level of expectation has risen. Now they want transistor radios, electric irons, bicycles, and other consumer goods which they previously never considered. Furthermore, while migrants are quick to point out that their own situation has improved after coming to Popayán, some are just as convinced that their fathers—at a similar age, working as peasant farmers—not only had a better standard of living than did the migrants when they left the countryside, but also lived better than do migrants today after they move to the city. These migrants feel that life in the countryside was less expensive in the old days and it was easier then than now to make a living tilling the soil. The majority, however, feel that their present circumstances are *better* than their fathers' and harbor no nostalgia for the past.

THE URBAN SCENE

The Tulcanés data do not support the belief that a breakdown in family life, personal maladjustment, a decline in religion, and an increase in juvenile delinquency, prostitution, and crime necessarily are concomitant with rural-urban movement (cf. Wirth 1938; Fried 1959). Rather, the Tulcán data more closely support findings made by those who note no real pressing adjustment problems among migrants to the cities (cf. Lewis 1952; Butterworth 1962; Mangin 1960; Mangin and Cohen 1964; Roberts 1973:13). The residents of Tulcán maintain that the transition from life in the country and adaptation to life in the city really are quite easy. There are several reasons for this.

First, the process of urbanization reaches out to the countryside. To a certain extent, the migrants know what to expect when they arrive in the city. Peasants, though partially autonomous, are constantly aware of their binding and often subservient relationships with urban centers and the state, which dictate many of their political, social, economic, and religious patterns of life (Foster 1967:8). For most of this century, national market systems have focused attention on peasants; the construction of roads facilitating peasant travel has enhanced mass media communications; the building and staffing of rural schools has produced literate peasants who have access to books, magazines, and newspapers.[2] Many Tulcaneses came from areas less than a day's bus ride from Popayán, and some lived as close as fifteen or twenty miles away. For years before moving to Popayán, these peasants brought their coffee to be sold at the Coffee Growers' Association, their sisal to Empaques del Cauca, and their surplus truck crops to the Friday market. In more recent years, the so-called transistor radio revolution has brought scores of heretofore isolated peasants into constant contact with an urban-based, urban-oriented national culture.[3] Furthermore, and very importantly, people who have migrated to cities return to visit relatives and to attend baptisms and local saint's days fiestas; during these visits they derive great satisfaction from explaining the ways of the city to their curious friends and relatives. Therefore, in many respects, the migrant to Popayán experiences no real surprises when he steps off the bus. The data seem to support findings of the Leeds, who write that a rural background is good preparation for life in the city (1970:233–34). Lisa R. Peattie notes in her study of migrants to

2. For an interesting discussion of modernization among Colombian peasants and the impact of mass media communications, see Rogers (1969), especially chapters 4 and 5.

3. Apparently this can produce negative results as well. Víctor Caicedo, M.D., who is a farmer and the founder of a small rural school, reports that he has noticed a decline in the literacy levels among Guambiano Indian peasant acquaintances near Silvia, Cauca. He attributes this decline to the introduction and availability of moderately priced transistor radios. Dr. Caicedo believes that many peasants no longer feel the need to attend classes, because with radios they are able to keep abreast of any news and have a source of constant entertainment close at hand.

the barrio of La Laja in Ciudad Guayana, Venezuela, that by the time migrants reach the city, they are "in some sense preadapted to urban life. One observer has called them a 'proto-proletariat'" (1968:118–19).

A second important factor in explaining why new Tulcaneses do not experience "breakdown" or "disorganization" when they arrive must be attributed, at least in part, to Popayán's size. Although Popayán is the capital of the Department of Cauca, a university city, and an ecclesiastical center, it possesses many small-town qualities. Popayán is a provincial capital, not a metropolis on the scale of Bogotá, Mexico City, or Buenos Aires. Its shopping district, which can be traversed by foot in minutes, lacks the frenzied excitement and movement of downtown Cali or Medellín. In this sense, Popayán has none of a big city's atmosphere of impersonality and intimidation. The country peasant in Popayán is usually not a complete country bumpkin, because the scale of things he encounters is one that he can grasp.

Third, the barrio itself has a rural, village-like atmosphere, and people find security in its small size. It has stores, a school, government, and a health center. In many respects, it probably differs little from the village where its residents were born. Women may spend very little time in the city, usually going only to its peripheral markets and perhaps walking to the center of town occasionally to deliver or bring back laundry. Many of the men have jobs which require little urban sophistication, and many work in the barrio itself. In a similar vein, Oscar Lewis points out that in Mexico City, "The *vecindad* acts as a shock absorber for the rural migrants to the city because of the similarity between its culture and that of the rural community" (1959:400).

Finally, the majority of migrants living in Tulcán had some assistance upon their arrival to Popayán. Many migrants had friends and relatives already living in Popayán when they arrived who often provided them with housing and, less frequently, found jobs for them. There are even stories about how people were assisted by complete strangers when they arrived. Angelina de Ordóñez recalls that when she arrived in Popayán twelve years ago with six children in tow, she knew no one. She spent her first day in town walking along the outskirts, looking for a place to stay. Finally a woman whom she had never seen before invited them to stay with her for a week. In 1959 Pedro Medina, his common-law wife, and seven other members of their extended family descended from a bus, hungry, dusty, and exhausted after a twenty-hour ride from Pasto, Nariño. By the time they had gathered their possessions and walked out of the bus terminal, they had been offered a free place to stay by a complete stranger. These cases are by no means unique. Thus, the new migrant often does not feel completely alone and helpless when he arrives in Popayán, for even without prior contacts, people find adjustment to urban life easy.

But once the adjustment to life in Tulcán is made, there is apparently no real need to seek out and maintain tight social networks with kin and friends, and there are virtually no voluntary associations. Except in cases of extended families living together, there is no clustering of households from the same vereda in the barrio. For example, very few of the eleven families from La Unión, Nariño, know each other, and most of the friendships between people from that community have been established since the individual families moved into the barrio; the two families from Barbacoas, Nariño, were united by fictive kin ties *after*, and not before, both families met in Tulcán.

MIGRANTS AND PAYANESES IN TULCÁN

In the barrio, differences in life styles between migrants and Payaneses appear to be few. The average Standard of Living Scores (to be discussed in chapter 4) for the two groups are approximately the same, and types of occupations and household incomes are equivalent. In matched ratings, both migrants and nonmigrants are listed among the richest and the poorest in the barrio. Both groups average about two years of primary school education, and their world views, medical beliefs and practices, and family structures are the same. Thus, it is difficult to distinguish the urban-born poor and the rural-born poor living in Tulcán: the barrio is a reservoir for similar people marked by the common denominator of poverty.

Living on the urban fringe does not necessarily mean that an urban ethos prevails among either group. Public opinion seems to be divided almost evenly on the "which-is-better-the-city-or-the-country" issue, with the votes that could make the difference specifically going to Tulcán because it exhibits both the advantages of the city (schools, medical facilities, and job possibilities other than agriculture) with those of the country (access to open spaces and freedom to grow crops and raise animals). "Rurbana," the fringe, appeals to most Tulcaneses, who feel that they are able to keep one foot in the city and one in the country.

3. Earning a Living

POPAYÁN is not an industrial center. The absence of industry, as we have seen, is not due to oversight by large companies, but rather to the conscious efforts of leading Payanés families, who derive their incomes from cattle ranching and do not wish to see Popayán become a large industrial center. Crist reports that Popayán's influential families actively discouraged industry from coming into the city and suggested that they locate in Cali instead (1950:137). Two decades later, he notes that industrial development and growth in the city still have changed very little (1971). This lack of industry, of course, greatly reduces the number of jobs available, resulting in a swollen labor force. Tulcaneses therefore find it difficult to obtain steady employment.

Their lack of marketable skills also adds to their difficulties in finding work. The great majority of Tulcanés migrant household heads were originally peasant farmers, and because of this rural background, most have had no nonagricultural training. Consequently, they are in a poor position to compete for the few skilled or semiskilled jobs which occasionally are available. Payanés-born residents are scarcely better off, for their levels of education and job training experience are similarly low.

Even with job training, people often are unable to find employment in the fields for which they are prepared. Héctor Arias spent nearly three years going at night to the Don Bosco trade school, learning to be an accountant. He finished the course, but was unable to get a job where he could utilize his new skills. Not one to give up easily, he enrolled a year or so later in the government-sponsored trade school Servicio Nacional de Aprendizaje (SENA) and completed a course in farm machinery maintenance. Much to his chagrin, Héctor once again was unable to find a job where he could put his learning to use, so he now divides his time between salting skins brought in from the stockyards and helping his father cultivate a large garden plot.

TULCANÉS OCCUPATIONS

Thus, Tulcaneses must rely on their own ingenuity to make a living, and consequently they have developed a wide variety of occupations. I have classified these jobs into thirteen categories, with an additional one for the unemployed (Table 3-1).

Small-scale commerce accounts for almost a quarter of the jobs of household heads. This is by far the broadest category with the widest spread of economic returns and possibilities, ranging from four households where each head earns 50 pesos or less per month to two households where each head makes between 1,000 and 1,500 pesos per month. Included in this group are the women who sell cooked food in the barrio and in the city markets, the produce vendors in the markets, and the people who sell candy and cigarettes from sidewalk stands around town. Similarly, the families that buy three-pound bundles of herbs and spices from the large food cooperatives in Popayán and carefully repackage the ingredients into small cellophane envelopes for resale are classed as small-scale merchants. Bakers, who work half the night preparing their wares and the following morning selling them, likewise come under this heading. The category also includes the numerous small-store owners in the barrio, whose goods range from a few commonly used items to practically everything Tulcaneses will need for any occasion.

Construction work accounts for the employment of 16.7

TABLE 3-1

Jobs and Incomes (in pesos): Household Heads Only

Job and % of Household Heads Represented	Lowest Income	Average Income	Highest Income
Small=scale commerce 22.5% (N=62)	$0–50	$384	$1,001–1,500
Construction 16.7% (N=46)	$101–200	$450	$1,001–1,500
Hauling[a] 9.8% (N=27)	$0–50	$248	$801–1,000
Government 9.8% (N=27)	$0–50	$674	$1,001–1,500
Agriculture[b] 8.4% (N=23)	$0–50	$162	$601–800
Unemployed 7.6% (N=21)	--	--	--
Other 7.3% (N=20)	$0–50	$464	$1,501–2,000
Housewife 4.7% (N=13)	--	--	--
Wash clothes 4.4% (N=12)	$0–50	$145	$401–500
Stockyard personnel 3.6% (N=10)	$101–200	$470	$801–1,000
Industry 2.2% (N=6)	$401–500	$800	$1,501–2,000
Clerks and waiters 1.8% (N=5)	$51–100	$365	$601–800
Tailor and seamstress 0.7% (N=2)	$51–100	$163	$201–300
Maid 0.4% (N=1)	$101–200	$150	$101–200

a. In hauling, as in most other categories, response is based on the assumption of ideal full-time and continuous employment.

b. Agriculturalists' incomes are misleading. They often have no idea what they earn, and they produce for themselves what others have to buy.

per cent of Tulcanés household heads. Since most building in the city is done with bricks and mortar, these men usually are masons or mason's helpers; they are free-lance workers who, when one project is finished, must search for work elsewhere. In the construction trade, an individual earns between 10 and 35 pesos a day for an average of approximately 450 pesos per month.

The general category of "hauling" is the third most common occupation, with approximately 10 per cent of household heads engaged full-time in this work. The terms *cotero*, *tersiador*, and *bultiador* are used to describe the men (and less frequently, the women) who push two-wheeled carts loaded with produce through the streets of town, or who unload cargo from buses and trucks. Three horse-drawn carts used for transporting freight are also based in Tulcán. Hauling, too, is free-lance; men leave their houses at six or six-thirty in the morning and head for the markets and warehouses in the city, where they stand around, talking and smoking, as they wait for customers. It is exhausting, heavy work with little financial reward (about 250 pesos per month). On good days, José Luís Muñoz may make 15 pesos; other times he brings home only 5 pesos, not unusual for men in this line of work. People age quickly in this profession; after working eight years as a hauler, José Rivera is permanently crippled and hunchbacked from the heavy loads with which he struggles daily.

Another 10 per cent of household heads work for branches of either the municipal or departmental government. Their occupations include road maintenance, garbage collection, and street sweeping. Any government job is highly desirable, for the work pays well, averaging between 650 and 700 pesos per month, and it includes many fringe benefits unavailable in other types of work.

Agriculture is the primary occupation of 8.4 per cent of household heads, and a secondary occupation of *most* Tulcaneses. Men like Jaime Arias, Jaime Istuasi, and Olimpo Castellanos are urban farmers who cultivate their plots of yuca, plantains, coffee, and a variety of garden vegetables. By selling herbs and vegetables to their neighbors, and by supplementing their incomes with wood brought down from the hills to be sold for cooking fuel, these men are able to make a living. Other agriculturalists work land outside the barrio. Some

FIGURE 2. Man inspecting his drying coffee, in poorest section of barrio. House on the right has walls of unmortared brick and split bamboo.

commute daily to small farms and return in the evening. Others, like Luís Martínez, leave their homes in the barrio early Monday morning and spend the week working on their farms, returning late Friday evening or early Saturday morning for the weekend. Still others, like Ever Astaiza and Jesús López, work nights in Popayán but try to spend at least one day a week on their farms, which are located in small villages within walking or cycling distance of Popayán. These agriculturalists should not be confused with other families whose primary source of income is derived outside of agriculture, but who have large gardens. A certain amount of farming is common to most Tulcaneses, and almost every family raises some produce for its own consumption.

The remaining household-head occupations are scattered among rather diverse jobs: there are clerks and waiters (1.8 per cent), a tailor and a seamstress (0.7 per cent), people who wash clothes (4.4 per cent), and stockyard personnel (3.6 per cent). The "other" category includes drivers, shoeblacks, night watchmen, prostitutes, and the like.

No professionals (such as lawyers, medical doctors, or teachers) live in the barrio, nor are there skilled craftsmen and petty artisans, which seem like natural job possibilities in a city with little industry. Although Popayán's city fathers are interested in attracting tourists, at present there is not enough demand for crafts to support a sizable number of artists. Tulcán does have a few tinsmiths and cobblers, but they are not really craftsmen and do not consider themselves to be such.

Unemployment[1] levels are difficult to estimate for several reasons. First, data from my interview, casual conversation, and observations indicate that both the jobs and incomes reported in the census sometimes reflect wishful thinking calculated on full-time employment and based on optimum earning levels, when actually the people involved were without jobs at

1. Urrutia reports that compared to the United States, unemployment is high even in Colombia's industrialized cities. From 1963 to 1965, the average minimum rate of unemployment in Bogotá was 7.1 per cent. In Medellín for the same period, it was 10.7 per cent, and in Cali, records kept for March–September 1965 showed an average minimum rate of 11.8 per cent unemployed (1968:3). He points out that because Colombia is a "developing" nation, at present its structural setup makes it literally impossible to obtain the goal of 3–4 per cent unemployed which the United States sets as a healthy level for its economy. Urrutia feels that Colombia would do well to reach a goal of 6–7 per cent unemployed (1968:38).

the time. Second, since most occupations are free-lance, employment is not steady for many, and nearly everyone spends a certain amount of time unemployed. And finally, most people not working at their chosen professions find piecemeal jobs, tend their gardens full-time, or chop wood to

TABLE 3-2

Jobs and Incomes (in pesos): All Household Members Combined

Job and % of Household Heads Represented	Lowest Household Income	Average Household Income	Highest Household Income
Small=scale commerce 22.5% (N=62)	$0-50	$607	$2,000 and up
Construction 16.7% (N=46)	$201-300	$645	$1,501-2,000
Hauling 9.8% (N=27)	$51-100	$419	$801-1,000
Government 9.8% (N=27)	$301-400	$875	$1,501-2,000
Agriculture 8.4% (N=23)	$0-50	$452	$1,501-2,000
Unemployed 7.6% (N=21)	$0-50	$351	$1,001-1,500
Other 7.3% (N=20)	$0-50	$576	$1,501-2,000
Housewife 4.7% (N=13)	$0-50	$483	$1,001-1,500
Wash clothes 4.4% (N=12)	$0-50	$308	$601-800
Stockyard personnel 3.6% (N=10)	$201-300	$550	$801-1,000
Industry 2.2% (N=6)	$401-500	$1,108	$1,501-2,000
Clerks and waiters 1.8% (N=5)	$51-100	$455	$601-800
Tailor and seamstress 0.7% (N=2)	$301-400	$400	$401-500
Maid 0.4% (N=1)	$101-200	$150	$101-200

sell to their neighbors. Thus, while they are unemployed as far as their nominal profession is concerned, they manage to keep busy and bring in at least some income. Hence, the job situation is more accurately characterized by underemployment[2] than by unemployment. For example, Pablo Arboleda said that he was a mason, yet for over a year, he did nothing but repackage herbs and spices with his wife and his mother. Rodolfo Aguirre described himself as a driver whenever he could find openings. Between times, however, he kept himself busy by running a very successful bicycle theft ring, in which he and a couple of cohorts stole bicycles from town, painted them, and trucked them south to the city of Pasto for sale there.

WORK-RELATED PROBLEMS

There are serious problems associated with the whole complex of work in Tulcán. One of these is the common practice among employers of underpaying workers. Because of the relatively large labor force, employers can pay very low wages and still have candidates willing to work. Most Tulcaneses feel they are lucky to get any type of job, regardless of how small the financial benefits are. Therefore, it is not unusual for a person to work thirty days a month, twelve hours a day, and to bring home less than half of what the Ministry of Labor of the Department of Cauca has designated as the minimum wage for such a category of work.[3]

The use of child labor is also common, and because many families find it necessary to send their children off to work, this is a tacitly accepted form of exploitation. Judith Ramírez, a thirteen-year-old girl, works a seventy-two-hour week carding wool in a small store where *ruanas* (Colombian ponchos) are woven. For this she earns 5 pesos a day. Her family sees this as a necessary addition to the family income, and they are not

2. The Colombian Council on Economic Development, working from the explanation used by the Colombian government's Bureau of Statistics, defines the underemployed as "those persons, even though working, who worked during the week [when the study was conducted] less than 32 hours and have been looking for more work" (CEDE 1968:302).

3. The Ministry of Labor of the department has drawn up guidelines for minimum pay, which ranges from 10 pesos per day for people engaged in agricultural work to 15 pesos per day for those working on construction sites with capital value of over 200,000 pesos. These guidelines were issued in September 1969 and by June 1971 had not been revised, even though inflation had caused the cost of living to spiral upward in the interim.

willing for her to quit in protest over poor wages and working conditions.

Tulcaneses also cite numerous cases of nonpayment for work done. Joaquín Saldarriaga's case is typical: he worked for ten days as a mechanic and driver for a teamster and was paid 15 pesos, a sum which did not even cover the cost of food on the trip. He was told that that was all the boss had and was told to return in a few days for the remainder. Joaquín went back twice, and after being sent away both times, realized he was never going to get his money.

Few receive the *prestaciones sociales* (employment social services), such as hospitalization and medical care, to which many are legally entitled and which should be paid for by monthly joint employer-employee contributions. Included in these services are the family subsidy from which the worker receives an extra percentage of his earnings for each child, the transportation subsidy which defrays some of the cost of getting to work, a retirement fund to which the employer pays one month's wages for every year the employee has worked, and a paid vacation based on the amount of time the individual has worked. Government-sponsored construction work, the local and regional government offices, and Empaques del Cauca provide some of these benefits. However, most employers do not, and the benefits are rarely considered as possibilities by employees. In some cases, the lack of these services is due solely to employer disregard for the law. In other instances—and this is true also in payment of the minimum legal wage—many small concerns, as most are in Popayán, would find it impossible to remain operational if they were to comply with the law.

The Ministry of Labor occasionally makes spot checks to determine if employers are obeying the law, but this produces mixed results. María Cruz was making 100 pesos per month working a seventy-two-hour week in a small candy factory which employed three girls. After what María believes was a visit by someone from the government, the establishment's owner announced that henceforth they were going to receive social security medical benefits, usually the first item employers will pay for. The following month, 19 pesos were deducted from María's pay. Calculated on the basis of what her minimum wage should have been (312 pesos per month), this would have been the correct amount; but because she was not receiving the minimum wage, the deduction amounted to a fifth of her salary. Medical service was not worth that much, and María's parents made her quit and look for work elsewhere.

Tulcaneses view legal recourse against labor injustices as totally unrealistic. When asked if complaints can be lodged against employers, Tulcaneses just shrug their shoulders and ask what good it would do. If the employee protests, he is likely to be fired; there are always people waiting for jobs.

TABLE 3-3

Number of Workers per Household

Number of Workers	Number of Households	% of Households
0	12	4.4
1	134	48.7
2	77	28.0
3	35	12.7
4	11	4.0
5	5	1.8
6	1	0.4

Manuel Calderón maintains that if an employee tried to make a complaint to a municipal official, he "would be called a Communist and thrown in jail." Colombia's two powerful labor unions, the Unión de Trabajadores Colombianos (Union of Colombian Workers) and the Confederación de Trabajadores Colombianos (Confederation of Colombian Workers), which should provide protection against labor abuses, are regarded by Tulcaneses as organizations which are not concerned with their plight and are in league, at least tacitly, with the upper class. While both the unions and the upper class probably would object to such a description, as far as most Tulcaneses are concerned it might as well be the case.

The poor feel that many government regulations discriminate against them rather than help them. They resent what they consider to be unnecessary legal requirements that must be fulfilled, just to apply for a job—such as blood tests and X-rays (at employee expense) to prove good health. Employees also need a 10-peso identification card and a 40-peso police good-conduct certificate. If a job applicant has been in trouble with the police, he must pay additional money to lawyers and officials to get a card. "Poor people like us," lamented Faustina de Arias, "can hardly afford all of these expenses." In addition, job seekers generally need two letters of recommendation from *personas honorables* (citizens in good standing who are known in the community) attesting to their character and trustworthiness. These are difficult for poor people to obtain and generally require influence with someone in the barrio who knows a third party who will write the letters. All of these items cost money, which—although this may amount to only 100 pesos—can prevent people from competing in the job market. Some may be able to get jobs where the various documents are not required by the employer, but this means they will not be paid very much.

Licensing of small businesses and sidewalk stands presents still another problem to Tulcaneses. Permits are required by law and may be revoked without warning for what Tulcaneses consider to be unfair, capricious, and illogical reasons. Micaela de Miranda felt discriminated against when the city made her close her cantina because it lacked adequate sanitary facilities. Even though most of the barrio is without a sewer and the existing sewer line does not run by her establishment, the health inspector closed the bar due to a violation of the city health regulations. Micaela fumed at this directive, feeling it to be just another example of how the poor are mistreated and abused. Furthermore, she was upset because she was one of the few cantina owners in the barrio to pay the municipal tax, and for that reason the authorities were able to locate her cantina and close down her operation. She believed the inspector would have settled for a bribe, but said she was too poor to pay off officials. Eventually her problem was solved when her husband spent two days digging a long trench and installing a urinal that was connected to the sewer line of a nearby street.

Thus, the Tulcanés workers see themselves as pawns in the work structure. They are ignored by the labor unions, underpaid, exploited by their employers, cheated of their earnings, and denied their rights. As far as they are concerned, the government does not care about the plight of the poor. On the contrary, Tulcaneses feel that not only does the government not enforce regulations established to protect the poor, but appears to enforce only those ordinances which harass them.

Although Tulcaneses feel abused and exploited, it is important to note that they have limits beyond which they will

TABLE 3-4

Percentage of People in Each Income Group

Income Group[a]	% of Households		% of Household Heads	
$0-50	7.3	(N=20)	16.7	(N=46)
$51-100	2.2	(N=6)	5.1	(N=14)
$101-200	8.7	(N=24)	12.7	(N=35)
$201-300	12.0	(N=33)	14.9	(N=41)
$301-400	8.0	(N=22)	11.3	(N=31)
$401-500	12.0	(N=33)	14.2	(N=39)
$501-600	11.6	(N=32)	9.1	(N=25)
$601-800	16.4	(N=45)	10.2	(N=28)
$801-1,000	9.1	(N=25)	2.5	(N=7)
$1,001-1,500	8.0	(N=22)	2.5	(N=7)
$1,501-2,000	4.4	(N=12)	0.7	(N=2)
$2,000 and up	0.4	(N=1)	-	

a. These income divisions were derived from responses recorded during my census of the 275 households in the Barrio Tulcán. The divisions were made as they were because of the large number of low incomes in the barrio.

not allow themselves to be mistreated. In several cases, people have given up good jobs for reasons of personal dignity. Jorge Cruz was on Popayán's police force for six years—a job he liked, with good pay and benefits. One day, after being humiliated unjustly by an officer in front of his entire unit, Jorge quit. He was unhappy to lose the benefits of being a policeman and says his present job not only pays less, but also has an element of instability; nevertheless, for reasons of honor, he felt he had no choice but to resign. Four years later, he is still bitter about the episode. Perhaps quitting for matters of principle is good for the pride of Tulcaneses who feel abused, but these are moves of consequence, as they must find other jobs—often not as good—in a flooded labor market.

WORKING WOMEN

As bleak as the labor situation appears for men in Tulcán, it is even gloomier for working women. Widowed, abandoned, or otherwise single women have very few job opportunities. Largely unskilled and more poorly educated than men, they must make a living for themselves, often while supporting a large brood of children. Some receive aid from kinsmen or have offspring who are old enough to make financial contributions, but these instances are more the exception than the rule. Because of financial difficulties, most of them share homes with other families, often having only a single room into which they must crowd with their children. They generally take in laundry or sell arepas, *masamora* (a corn and sugar broth), and other cooked foods. Some make their living bringing wood down from the hills and selling it to barrio stores. Others manage to keep going by picking raspberries and cutting flowers which they sell in the markets and on the streets in Popayán. Most do a combination of these things and send their children to beg in Popayán. Some turn to prostitution.

Margarita Chávez is single, and although she is only twenty-nine years old, she looks forty. Life has not been easy for her. At the age of fifteen, unmarried, she had her first child. Now, fourteen years later, she has eleven children living with her. They survive on what the children bring home from begging and what she makes washing clothes and as a prostitute. Luz Benavides is eighteen years old and unmarried. She lives with her two daughters, ages four and two, and four half-brothers and half-sisters, ranging in age from thirteen to six, in a one-room, dirt-floored hovel. Luz and her thirteen-year-old half-sister make tamales and in this manner earn approximately 150 pesos a month. The other children beg. The plight of the urban poor is thus accentuated in the case of women.

ATTITUDES TOWARD WORK

It is not surprising that a considerable gap exists in Tulcanés attitudes between real and ideal work situations and types of employment. Tulcaneses would prefer to have nonmanual labor jobs, for they are more prestigious and almost by definition carry with them higher monetary rewards than does manual labor. Tulcaneses also see a positive correlation between Payaneses who work in offices and those who at least appear to have financial comfort and security. They believe that nonmanual labor is far less taxing on the body, and that because of this, life is made easier.

Tulcaneses say that people should work at whatever they want. The general attitude among adults of both sexes is summed up by Hernán Sánchez: "People should learn work they like. If they do not like it, they will not learn and will not work." It is significant that the residents of Tulcán feel this way since they are at the lower end of Popayán's socioeconomic continuum, their occupational roles for all intents and purposes are ascribed, and their possibilities for change are minimal.

When I asked how they thought they could improve their situation, they admitted that their only chance for improvement would be to move from a lower-paying job to a higher-paying job, and that this would be possible only within the range of occupations which members of their community presently share. That is, they feel that they could never become lawyers, teachers, or clerks in one of the local banks. Tulcaneses believe that their chances for any kind of real improvement are negligible because those in power need an abundant supply of cheap labor; thus, the system purposely holds them where they are.

Tulcanés children acquire an early concern for their situation, as revealed in short essays on career aspirations written by the twenty-six third-graders (seven girls, nineteen boys) of the Barrio Tulcán elementary school. Both sexes wrote about the importance of helping to support their poor families and beseeched assistance from the Almighty in doing this. The girls all wanted to become either a nun or a teacher. For most boys, being a driver was the favorite choice, reflecting a preference for "nonmanual" labor, while most others indicated a desire to work in construction. In these essays, the belief was often expressed that it takes money to make money, which was probably a way of saying, "This will never happen to me." A representative essay read like Pedro Londoño's: "If God gives me life, and if I am able to make money, I would like to be a driver in order to help my family which is so poor."

In spite of their difficulties in obtaining work, Tulcaneses have an interesting work ethic. Except for the very young and very old, the physically and mentally infirm, and those going to school, everyone is expected to make a contribution to the household. While residents express sympathy for themselves and their neighbors who have particularly difficult or unpleasant jobs, they do not feel sorry for anyone who does not work and who complains about not finding a job. Tulcaneses are convinced that anyone can find some kind of work if he is determined. People who use a difficult job market as an excuse simply are dismissed as irresponsible.

4. Standards of Living
and Economic Life in Tulcán

HAVING EXAMINED the employment situation and the various jobs open to Tulcaneses, I now turn to a discussion of the kind of living their efforts provide—specifically, the availability and use of municipal public services, standards of living and material possessions, spending priorities, and buying, credit, and saving patterns.

PUBLIC SERVICES IN TULCÁN

Although the barrio has a number of public services, their effectiveness is not what it should or could be. City water service is available, and 84 per cent of the households have it, at a minimum monthly rate of 5 pesos. Since there are no community faucets, families that do not have access to municipal water must carry what they need from two small natural springs located in the southwest corner of the barrio. The sewer network is perfunctory at best, with only a quarter of the households having access to the lines. Many families do not use the system because of the expense of making a connection and the poor performance of the sewer. Nearly half of all families have latrines in their backyards, and over a quarter are without sanitary services of any kind.

Electricity is inexpensive, and nearly half of the barrio households have it, although its use generally is limited to a single bare light bulb and perhaps a radio. Electrical power in the barrio is 220 volts rather than the 110 voltage of Popayán, an inconvenience for those with appliances, which are generally 110 volts. Frequent power failures coupled with insufficient voltage, which produces little more than a faint glow of electric light at peak hours of use, severely reduce the effectiveness and desirability of having electricity. Still, it is a highly prestigious item, a primary reason for its widespread use. In spite of the poor quality of these public services, barrio residents proudly point out that some of the other barrios around Popayán, including those which are not so poor, lack them.

At present there is no municipal bus service in the barrio, and the only alternative for those without bicycles is to rely on taxi drivers, who charge high prices because they feel that the roads in Tulcán damage their cabs. There are plans to extend service to the barrio, a great improvement for Tulcaneses who must walk to and from Popayán, often carrying heavy loads; but to date the barrio Junta has been unsuccessful in accomplishing this. Spokesmen for the company, whose lines terminate a kilometer from the barrio, say that the community must widen and strengthen the bridge leading into Tulcán and improve the condition of its streets before buses can make the circular route through the barrio. Thus, it will be some time before these plans are realized.

HOUSING AND MATERIAL POSSESSIONS

Tulcaneses do not have numerous material possessions, and what they have are characterized more by utilitarian qualities than by prestige attributes. Nevertheless, the items which they do have tell us certain things about their lives (cf. Lewis 1969, 1970).

Barrio houses resemble each other in that they are all single-story and of a quality below that of most of the others in Popayán. Beyond that, there is considerable variation in house construction and possessions.

Many of the poorest families live in one-room shacks with dirt floors and windowless sides made of bamboo, cane, and cardboard, and a roof made of flattened metal barrels and olive

FIGURE 3. Some of Barrio Tulcán's poorest houses. Roofs are a combination of corrugated asphalt sheets, discarded metal, and tile; walls are made of bamboo.

oil tins. Hernán and Lucilia Granada and their six children live in such a dwelling, measuring 10 by 18 feet. Their few clothes are stored in metal cans or wedged between the cane and cardboard siding. Two wooden beds without mattresses take up most of the house's interior. The walls are devoid of any decorations. The house has a solid wooden door, but it lacks a knob or lock and is flimsily held in place by two undersized hinges. On the floor next to the door is the wood cooking fire, with a few pots and pans left around it because they are the only items in the house the rats will not destroy.

At the other end of the housing scale are dwellings with three or more rooms and concrete-and-tile floors. These houses have windows, usually with glass panes, and the walls are brick covered with stucco. Their sloping roofs are made of the same clay tiles that give Popayán its cherished colonial appearance. They have electricity, water, and sewer connections. The house of Adolfo and Rosa Samboni provides a good example of houses at the upper end of the continuum. Their living room is furnished with a couch, three stuffed chairs, a coffee table, a radio, and a record player. The walls of the house are graced with the colorful calendars and religious artwork common in many Tulcanés homes. Rosa cooks in the kitchen on a double-burner kerosene stove. With good reason, their neighbors regard the Sambonis as one of the most "accommodated," i.e., well-to-do, families in the barrio.

Most Tulcanés houses fall somewhere between these two extremes. Walls often are part brick and part wattle-and-daub, and roofs may be combinations of tin and corrugated sheets of roofing asphalt. Floors are either cement, brick, tile, or a combination. The average house has three rooms and one paneless, almost permanently shuttered window facing the street. The chances of its having electricity are almost fifty-fifty. There are 6.4 people living in the house and about half as many beds as people. Cooking is done on wood fires or one- or two-burner kerosene stoves; many houses have both. The latrine and water spigot are located behind the house. There the family raises herbs and vegetables, as well as bananas, coffee, and flowering plants. The average household has a couple of chickens and, more than likely, a dog, kept as a watchdog and protector rather than a pet.

By official Colombian standards, the quality of Tulcanés

housing is considerably below par. The Instituto de Crédito Territorial, in a survey of Tulcanés housing conducted in October 1969, classified 30.3 per cent of Tulcanés houses as in good condition; 29.2, mediocre; and 40.5, bad (ICT 1970:2).

The clothes which Tulcaneses buy are unstylish, and cheap in quality and price. Some young women are very aware of fashions and dress in colorful, inexpensive miniskirts and bell-bottom slacks, but most women wear dark dresses or skirts and blouses almost indistinguishable from each other in their drabness. Tulcanés men do not have "work clothes" as such; they use the oldest and most dilapidated of their dark cotton slacks and plain, light-colored sport shirts for work. Although heavy-duty work shoes are available for between 70 and 90 pesos (about $3.50 to $4.50 U.S.), for aesthetic reasons they are rejected in favor of comparably priced dress shoes which are worn on construction sites and in wet, muddy fields. Only one individual in the barrio still wears *alpargatas* (fiber-soled sandals), a type of footwear which residents claim was almost universal among the poor a decade ago. Most barrio children go barefoot, although many have shoes which are saved for special occasions.

One indication of Tulcanés poverty is the amount and condition of their clothing. Changes of clothes appear to be limited to a couple of sets of worn-out apparel, at times resembling patchwork quilts when different pieces of material overlap until the original fabric is lost among the additions. Broken zippers cause women to tug at their dresses repeatedly in an effort to keep their shoulders covered. However, the women spend hours washing clothes, and they are well-scrubbed and well-mended, even if threadbare.

Tulcaneses purchase their clothing from vendors in and around the central market, or from shopkeepers whose businesses are located on the fringe of Popayán's downtown shopping district. They also can have inexpensive clothes made by any of the numerous seamstresses and tailors in town. Since charitable organizations, such as CARE and the Catholic groups Acción Católica and Caritas, distribute used clothing from the United States, it is not unusual to see children wearing sweatshirts with "Harvard University" or "Green Bay Packers" stenciled on their fronts.

Most Tulcanés possessions represent large capital investments, even when they are purchased second-hand. The major portion of these goods are utilitarian, and many of them are used in the owner's occupation. Thirty per cent of the households have bicycles, virtually the only form of transportation that may be purchased by the poor. Although these are not purchased as prestige items, they soon become *objets d'art*, since after their purchase they are covered with decals of Che Guevara, Donald Duck, and catchy slogans. The two barrio automobiles, a 1951 Chevrolet and a 1946 Dodge, are owned by taxi drivers, who purchased them second-hand; although both are in poor mechanical condition, they represent investments of 15,000 to 20,000 pesos apiece (between $750 and $1,000 U.S.).

The thirty sewing machines—none electric—in the barrio are used for business, and their owners work either full-time or part-time as seamstresses or tailors. The barrio's four refrigerators are in stores. They are not used for the storage of family food, but rather for salable items: the lower compartments are filled with beer and soft drinks, while the freezer contains homemade *paletas* (frozen fruit-flavored ices).

The radios, televisions, and record players are the only items purchased for their entertainment and prestige value. There are 161 radios in the barrio, and about 60 per cent of the households have them. During the day, these radios are played constantly at a volume loud enough for everyone in the house, as well as many of the neighbors, to hear. The 21 record players are very prestigious and expensive items and are in great demand for parties.

For a while there were two television sets in the barrio. One was repossessed, but the other still continues to serve as a source of entertainment and prestige to its owners, the Velascos, who in late afternoon unshutter their front window so that a small crowd can gather outside to watch soap operas.

Tulcaneses are inveterate and omnifarious collectors; they never throw away pieces of paper larger than a cigarette wrapper, and old bottles and tin cans are stored away carefully for use at a later time.

STANDARDS OF LIVING

In an attempt to categorize economic status of households, a Standard of Living Score has been devised, with a 20-point scale based on items which are not absolutely necessary to existence.[1] Two points are awarded for electricity, sewer or latrine, tile floors, and electric or propane stoves. Except for the number of rooms, for which no points are given, the rest of the items listed in Table 4-1 carry a 1-point value. In instances where a household possesses cement-and-tile floors or both a kerosene and an electric stove, points are assigned only for the item with the highest value.

Of the total of 275 households, 10 have a score of zero points. Eighty-two households score from 1 to 5 points; 130 households, 6 to 10 points; 48 households, 11 to 15 points; and 5 households, 16 or 17 points (the highest scores assigned). The average Standard of Living Score is 7.3 points per household (Table 4–2).

The following interrelationships shed light on factors that affect the Standard of Living Scores. The number of workers in a household does not show a positive relationship with the Standard of Living Score, but there is a correlation between the score and the household income, and, similarly, between the score and the income of the household head. Not surprisingly, then, as the household income or household-head income increases, the Standard of Living Score also tends to increase. Having a literate household head positively correlates with the Standard of Living Score, as does an increase in the household head's number of years of school. There is an even stronger positive correlation between the general educational level and the household's score.

Payanés-born people have a slightly higher Standard of Living Score than do migrants, with 53 per cent of the native-born registering a score above 7, in contrast to only 45 per cent of the migrants. In housing, as one might expect, squatters as a group (N=9) have the lowest score, averaging only 1.6 (as opposed to 7.3 for Tulcaneses as a whole). Renters (N=84) also rate below the norm with an average score of 6.2, while homeowners (N=182) average 8.1.

Households headed by women (N=47) have a slightly lower score than do those headed by men (N=228). Undoubtedly this difference has to do with the types of jobs women can get, which affect their earnings and spending power.

1. The Standard of Living Scale is modeled after Foster's point system for classification of houses in Tzintzuntzan, Mexico (Foster 1967:48–50).

TABLE 4-1

Household Item Frequency

Item	% of Households	Number of Households
One room	11.3	31
Two rooms	32.0	88
Three rooms	29.5	81
Four or more rooms	27.3	75
Water	83.6	230
Brick, cement, or tile floors	67.7	186
Kerosene, electric, or propane stoves	61.8	170
Radio	58.5	161
Latrine	46.2	127
Electricity	45.5	125
Electric iron	34.5	95
Bicycle	29.8	82
Sewer and indoor toilet	25.8	71
Glass windows	14.2	39
Sewing machine	10.9	30
Record player	7.6	21
Refrigerator	1.5	4
Car	0.7	2
Television	0.4	1

TABLE 4-2

Distribution of Standard of Living Scores

Scale Score	Number of Households	Percentage
00	10	3.6
01	5	1.8
02	21	7.6
03	14	5.1
04	18	6.5
05	24	8.7
06	27	9.8
07	27	9.8
08	22	8.0
09	29	10.5
10	25	9.1
11	11	4.0
12	16	5.8
13	7	2.5
14	9	3.3
15	5	1.8
16	3	1.1
17	2	0.7
18	--	--
19	--	--
20	--	--
Total	275	99.7

There is no correlation between the Standard of Living Score and increasing age of the household head, perhaps indicating that wisdom and experience matter little in obtaining the material comforts in life. Tulcaneses, very much aware of this, look upon offspring as their form of old age social security.

DAILY EXPENSES

In an effort to better understand the economic life of Tulcaneses, I asked eight families to itemize their daily income and expenditures. These budgets were kept for periods ranging from six weeks to ten months. The following discussion is based primarily on data from the budgets of four families for fifteen weeks, shown in Tables 4–3 to 4–6. These four families are representative of the economic continuum in the barrio and include one of the poorest families, one of the most "comfortable," and two with intermediate incomes.

In every case, food is the greatest single expense, requiring an average 70 per cent of incomes (Table 4–7). The Granada family, for example, spends less money—an average of 46.20 pesos per week, or 5.80 pesos per person—on food than do any of the others, while its average weekly income is 66.65 pesos, also the lowest. The Soto family spends the most on food, averaging 164.20 pesos weekly, or 41.05 pesos per person, out of an average income of 246.05 pesos. Starchy foods like potatoes, yuca, plantains, and bread are cheap and most commonly purchased. Fruits and vegetables rank second in frequency of purchase, while meat is a luxury item. Table 4–8 shows prices of items commonly purchased.

Household supplies, such as soap, candles, kerosene, and wood, account for approximately another tenth of the family budget.

The miscellaneous category, which comprises 6.8 per cent of expenditures, consists of such transactions as repayment of loans and debts, claiming property from pawnshops, and occasional purchases of school supplies. Rent payment is classified as a miscellaneous expenditure.

Entertainment accounts for a mere 2.1 per cent of the sample budgets, and from observations and discussions, this percentage appears to be quite representative of the barrio as a whole. Most of this money is spent on beer (1.20 pesos per

TABLE 4-3

Weekly Expenses and Income of the Nemecio Gonzáles Family (in pesos)

Week No.	Total Expenses	Food	Clothes	Medical	Household Supplies	Transp.	Entertainment	Misc.	Util.	Income
1	381.50	182.95	--	19.30	10.70	0.90	49.55	47.50	72.00	357.00
2	291.00	143.00	--	8.00	22.90	10.40	52.00	103.00	--	470.00
3	310.95	134.20	22.00	15.10	40.95	1.40	63.20	24.10	10.00	415.00
4	378.30	141.55	118.00	--	18.55	7.00	25.10	67.20	--	313.00
5	255.50	130.40	--	2.00	21.10	50.20	14.20	37.60	--	267.00
6	286.50	154.85	10.00	--	15.95	4.00	14.10	87.60	--	220.00
7	364.80	138.50	13.00	21.00	35.20	20.40	46.50	90.20	--	447.00
8	186.50	127.00	1.30	4.50	16.40	3.20	11.70	22.40	--	20.00
9	176.75	96.45	--	1.00	18.90	21.10	1.00	38.40	--	445.00
10	525.90	279.00	56.50	7.50	38.60	24.00	23.70	98.60	--	365.50
11	246.20	112.80	101.50	3.50	9.00	5.00	4.00	10.40	--	248.00
12	844.90	248.60	325.70	20.00	40.30	7.00	37.80	55.50	110.00	860.00
13	168.40	152.10	--	--	2.40	4.40	0.20	9.30	--	100.00
14	769.75	181.25	313.30	11.70	55.80	1.60	39.30	166.80	--	792.00
15	497.65	210.85	35.00	0.50	9.20	8.80	32.00	201.30	--	290.00
Total	5,684.60	2,433.50	996.30	114.10	355.95	169.40	414.35	1,059.90	192.00	5,609.50
% of Expenses	100%	42.8%	17.5%	2.0%	6.3%	3.0%	7.3%	18.6%	3.4%	

TABLE 4-4

Weekly Expenses and Income of the Francisco Soto Family (in pesos)

Week No.	Total Expenses	Food	Clothes	Medical	House-hold Supplies	Transp.	Enter-tainment	Misc.	Util.	Income
1	161.30	161.30	--	--	--	--	--	--	--	65.20
2	160.90	157.10	--	--	--	--	--	3.80	--	297.60
3	146.90	146.90	--	--	--	--	--	--	--	202.00
4	179.30	170.40	--	--	5.10	--	--	3.80	--	254.00
5	166.90	160.40	--	--	4.60	--	--	1.90	--	125.00
6	165.90	154.40	--	--	5.50	--	--	--	6.00	174.00
7	151.30	151.30	--	--	--	--	--	--	--	178.00
8	159.00	159.00	--	--	--	--	--	--	--	196.00
9	170.40	165.80	--	--	4.60	--	--	--	--	165.00
10	165.10	165.10	--	--	--	--	--	--	--	252.00
11	175.00	170.60	--	--	2.50	--	--	1.90	--	150.00
12	173.50	172.70	--	--	0.80	--	--	--	--	196.00
13	177.90	177.90	--	--	--	--	--	--	--	167.00
14	176.00	176.00	--	--	--	--	--	--	--	208.00
15	400.10	174.10	--	--	226.00	--	--	--	--	1,061.00
Total	2,729.50	2,463.00	--	--	249.10	--	--	11.40	6.00	3,690.80
% of Expenses	100%	90.2%	--	--	9.1%	--	--	0.4%	0.2%	

TABLE 4-5

Weekly Expenses and Income of the Samuel Méndez Family (in pesos)

Week No.	Total Expenses	Food	Clothes	Medical	House-hold Supplies	Transp.	Enter-tainment	Misc.	Util.	Income
1	124.40	78.10	7.50	--	26.60	--	1.30	10.90	--	124.70
2	114.70	86.00	--	--	13.70	--	2.60	12.40	--	126.30
3	180.50	108.45	11.80	--	27.30	--	--	32.95	--	180.50
4	132.25	102.15	0.70	--	22.90	--	1.00	5.50	--	120.50
5	119.10	82.25	9.00	--	10.85	--	3.00	14.00	--	106.00
6	108.40	83.40	--	--	13.40	--	0.40	11.20	--	107.10
7	122.75	84.75	--	--	24.50	--	4.00	9.50	--	132.00
8	161.35	107.00	--	2.00	16.85	--	5.00	30.50	--	159.90
9	180.30	119.60	--	4.25	13.80	--	1.70	40.95	--	171.50
10	115.45	96.15	--	--	17.30	--	--	2.00	--	111.00
11	176.30	119.65	--	--	20.40	--	--	36.25	--	176.00
12	121.55	100.05	--	--	17.75	--	--	3.75	--	98.00
13	160.35	129.65	--	--	16.20	--	--	14.50	--	210.50
14	161.05	126.30	--	2.00	15.90	--	--	16.85	--	138.50
15	154.45	125.95	--	--	23.80	--	--	4.70	--	165.50
Total	2,132.90	1,549.45	29.00	8.25	281.25	--	19.00	245.75	--	2,128.00
% of Expenses	100%	72.6%	1.4%	0.4%	13.2%	--	0.9%	1.1%	--	

TABLE 4-6

Weekly Expenses and Income of the Hernán Granada Family (in pesos)

Week No.	Total Expenses	Food	Clothes	Medical	Household Supplies	Transp.	Entertainment	Misc.	Util.	Income
1	31.05	25.65	--	--	4.90	--	--	1.10	--	19.00
2	49.40	38.70	--	--	9.20	--	--	1.50	--	40.50
3	103.30	36.55	--	50.00	7.50	--	--	9.25	--	109.00
4	43.25	35.85	--	--	5.30	--	--	2.10	--	56.00
5	63.75	47.45	--	--	5.90	--	--	10.40	--	73.00
6	57.60	50.20	--	--	5.90	--	--	1.50	--	92.00
7	54.45	47.15	--	--	5.50	--	--	1.80	--	66.10
8	67.25	52.20	--	4.00	8.80	--	--	2.25	--	68.00
9	41.65	36.75	--	--	3.40	--	--	1.50	--	69.00
10	62.85	49.35	--	--	10.50	--	--	3.00	--	63.00
11	61.95	54.40	--	--	6.20	--	--	1.35	--	67.00
12	68.45	51.90	--	--	5.80	--	--	10.75	--	68.00
13	69.45	56.60	--	--	10.10	--	--	2.75	--	61.00
14	86.45	59.75	--	--	16.70	--	--	10.00	--	69.00
15	65.65	50.30	--	4.00	9.60	--	--	5.75	--	79.00
Total	926.50	692.80	--	58.00	115.30	--	--	65.00	--	999.60
% of Expenses	100%	74.8%	--	6.3%	12.4%	--	--	7.0%	--	--

bottle) and various types of hard liquor, such as aguardiente (8 pesos per bottle) and rum (15 pesos per bottle). Betting at the cockfights and going to movies are among the favorite recreational pastimes of Tulcaneses, and comprise most of the other entertainment expenditures.

In summary, the buying of food consumes the major portion of Tulcaneses' incomes. Much of what is left goes toward the acquisition of other items directly connected with the household's functioning, such as soap, wood, and candles.

TABLE 4-7

Average Percentage of Budgets of Four
Families Spent in Each Category

Food	70.1
Household supplies	10.3
Miscellaneous	6.8
Clothing	4.7
Medical	2.2
Entertainment	2.1
Utilities	0.9
Transportation	0.8

What remains is used for clothing, for medical expenses, and other necessities of life, leaving little—if anything—for entertainment or recreational purposes.

BUYING, CREDIT, AND SAVINGS

Food shopping follows an almost ritual pattern. Usually early in the morning while fresh supplies are still plentiful, barrio women walk to Popayán's main market facing the Parque Mosquera, or to the smaller Barrio Alfonso López market, which is less distant but also has less variety. There they purchase the day's requirements of meat, vegetables, fruits, and other fresh produce. Dry staples such as rice, sugar, coffee, and salt are purchased as needed throughout the day in Tulcán stores, and children, rather than women, usually make these short trips.

This daily shopping pattern is determined by several factors. First, there are no refrigerators except in four stores, so perishables can be kept for only a short time. There is usually

TABLE 4-8

Food Prices (in pesos)

Meat	6.00–10.00 per lb.
Rice	2.00 per lb.
Sugar	1.00 per lb.
Potatoes	0.50 per lb.
Envelope of coffee (4 cups)	0.30 each
Peas	6.00–8.00 per lb.
Bread rolls	0.15–0.20 each
Yuca	0.20 each
Bananas	1.00 per bunch of four
Plantains	0.50 each
Oranges	0.10 each
Chicken	40.00 each
Guinea pig	10.00–15.00 each

little storage space in houses even for nonperishables, and even if a woman were able to carry a week's supply of groceries from a distant market. Moreover, when family heads are paid on a daily basis, there is usually not enough cash in the house to make purchases for several days in the future. And even those few men who are paid good wages every fortnight usually give to their wives only enough for a day's purchases. Finally, women enjoy daily shopping expeditions, for they break the monotony at home and provide opportunity to socialize with neighbors during the walk to and from town.

Like many Latin American residential areas, Barrio Tulcán has numerous (N=41) small housefront stores which sell almost everything necessary for a barrio household. Competition is intense since most stores sell the same items. Yet many Tulcaneses show distinct preferences for some stores over others, even if it means walking half-way across the barrio to buy a package of cigarettes. Marta de Cruz no longer shops in her cousin's store because she found out that he charged 10 centavos more for a package of Alka Seltzer than did another store owner slightly farther away. Marta felt her cousin should, if anything, sell things to her for less than the competitor. Jaime Arias does not shop at the store nearly adjacent to his house because the store owners play their radio late at night and otherwise engage in "scandalous behavior." Instead he goes to a store where he has made an arrangement to exchange for supplies the wood he and his family bring down from the hills. Primitivo Aguirre attracts customers to his store because of a unique service he offers: in addition to selling standard commodities, he rents comic books—20 centavos if the comic books are read at the store, 30 centavos if the customer takes them home.

Ward (1960) has suggested that a bazaar-type economy with many small stores selling the same things functions to provide credit, each store carrying a small number of creditors. This does not seem to be the case in Tulcán. Credit is not encouraged, and when stores do extend it, they do so reluctantly and to a very few select customers. Store owners demand that bills be paid within the week, often adding a 10 per cent service charge. Most people agree with store owner Hernándo López, who says simply, "They don't ask and I don't offer." As Micaela de Miranda observes, "You can see their faces, but not their hearts." Although Jaime Torres has lived in the barrio for five years, only recently has he started to receive credit in a store, and then only after he and the owner established fictive kinship ties. Referring to other stores in the barrio, Jaime notes, "If I went in I wouldn't get 5 centavos in credit."

Barrio store owners maintain that the refusal to give credit is the only way they can remain in business. They note that families can come and go in a matter of hours and so there is really no way to collect bills once a loan is made or credit is extended. There are no old families whose members have intermarried and known each other for generations, no customs and rules for interpersonal relationships passed down through the years to regulate interaction, and few long-term, stable social networks. As most people realize, life in Tulcán is lived in an every-man-for-himself environment.

The story of Adolfo Gonzáles provides a good case study of the problems of giving credit. Shortly after his arrival in the summer of 1970, Adolfo began selling fruits and vegetables at the barrio entrance. He observed that there was really nothing resembling a miniature market in the barrio and reasoned that he might earn a good living by saving women the trip to Popayán. In the beginning Adolfo's market was financially sound: business was good, and within a fortnight it had expanded so successfully that he moved to a larger site complete with a protective canvas canopy shadowing himself and his products.

In an effort to build up a clientele, Adolfo began giving credit to barrio women: "I wanted to show the people that I was interested in helping the barrio and would trust them." Much to his chagrin, Adolfo found that people did not repay their debts. After buying on credit, they simply avoided his stand, and within a couple of weeks his working capital was reduced by over 150 pesos. After several months, it became clear that the venture was going to be a financial disaster, but he continued with money sent to him by his son from the family farm. Finally, when his capital was nearly exhausted, Adolfo left the stand to the care of his nine-year-old son Jaime and went to look for work in Popayán.

Those who need money, not credit, turn either to one of the barrio's money lenders, who charge 10 per cent interest per month (7 per cent to good friends), or to store owners who (although reluctant to advance credit) will make small loans of 5 to 10 pesos to people they know well. Several individuals told me that the Junta occasionally makes small loans to needy families, but I knew of no one who had received this assistance. The persistent economic insecurity that Tulcaneses face forces many of them to patronize La Amiga and La Cordialidad, two of Popayán's pawn shops. Thus, bicycles, electric irons, and radios are shuttled back and forth between the barrio and one of the two shops, as the need arises. Patrons are charged 7 per cent monthly on the loan and have six months to reclaim their merchandise before it is put up for sale. In this way, material goods of practically any value serve as protection against complete financial disaster. Families are very careful to make sure they do not lose sales slips or other proof of ownership so that they may use these items as collateral in pawn shops.

Some families look upon the raising of animals—guinea pigs, chickens, ducks, and especially pigs—as a form of insurance which they can cash in at any time. Piglets represent an initial investment of 300–400 pesos; when full-grown, they can be sold for up to 12,000 pesos. Most families let their pigs forage in barrio streets, rounding them up only at night to prevent theft or loss. For these owners, the first financial investment is the last. Others, however, like Matilda Gómez, make an effort to fatten their pigs by feeding them fruit skins, corn, and other vegetable wastes. Eva de Angulo proudly points out that she was able to buy her land in the barrio with the money from the sale of one pig. Thus, for the poor, keeping a hog or two is the equivalent of money in the bank.

Never knowing when they will be sick or out of work, families try to save money whenever they can. After food and other household necessities are purchased, any remaining money is wadded up in an old cloth and wedged out of sight in a hole in the wall or placed in a jar in a dark corner of the kitchen. Some families have savings accounts in Popayán and try to make regular deposits of 5 or 10 pesos. Thus, material goods, animals, and savings all provide Tulcaneses with some measure of economic security.

5. Social Relations

Tulcanés Perspective

Tulcán is a lower-class barrio; both the barrio inhabitants and the people living in Popayán agree that it is the poorest of the city's barrios. Officially, it is classified as a slum. Tulcaneses call themselves "humble people," "poor people," or members of the "lower class," and they call Tulcán a "poor barrio," "popular barrio," or "worker's barrio." These terms are also used by other Payaneses when referring to Tulcán, and they are the designations for Tulcán which appear both in the local newspaper and in the official literature.

SOCIAL CLASS

In looking at overall social structure, Tulcaneses do not see a continuum of social classes; rather, they view society as polarized, consisting of "them"—anybody who is not as poor as they themselves are—and "us"—the residents of Tulcán and Popayán's other poor barrios. Tulcaneses view life as a continuous struggle, one in which people must "defend" themselves and must "fight" with the myriad forces of life in a constant effort to survive, a conception which is carried over to their model of social classes. The poor, they feel, have little or no control over their destiny.[1] Naturally, this realization produces discontent, a feeling which is far from new among the poor but which has increased in recent years because many of them are no longer convinced that their position in life is something willed by God; it is now therefore subject to change. This new attitude is due to improved media communications which expose the poor to new thoughts and ideas, prompted in part by a changing attitude of the ruling aristocracy (cf. A. Whiteford 1970). This, in turn, has served to create a sense of frustration and resentment among the poor at their inability to make what they feel is sufficient headway toward meeting these now-rising expectations.[2]

Under these circumstances, it is not surprising that Tulcaneses feel life is a fight against a conscious conspiracy perpetrated against them by the "oligarchy" which wishes to maintain its power and can do so only by keeping the "common people" from ever really asserting themselves. To Tulcaneses the term "oligarch" means anyone who they believe has a vested interest in maintaining the status quo—obviously not a complimentary or endearing term. This feeling of being restrained or held down by the rich extends to every area of their lives. Thus, when Tulcaneses talk about their plight, which they refer to as *la lucha* ("the fight"), they frequently use a gesture like a basketball dribble to illustrate how the oligarchy keeps them down.

Further, they say that their poverty forces them into situations they would not have to face if they were rich, and they assume that their lives are controlled both directly and indirectly by the rich. Hence, when Lupe de Martínez' son-in-law was jailed on charges of robbing a drunk, she was very perturbed. After a trip to the jail, she decided that it was a clear case of harassment of the poor. If her son-in-law had been rich, she argued, he never would have been arrested, or

1. This is not an unusual reaction from members of the lower class. Referring to lower-class coastal Colombians, Whitten notes a similar feeling of powerlessness among them: "[The] power of lower class persons over the events influencing their well-being is minimal vis-à-vis other groups" (1969:228–29).

2. Andrew Whiteford noted a change in attitude among urban lower-class individuals from Barrio Alfonso López between 1952 and 1962. There was "considerably more tension, frustration, and expressed antagonism toward the status quo than I ever encountered before" (1963:17).

if by some remote chance he had been, a few well-placed pesos would have settled the issue quickly and quietly. Even after Ernesto confessed to the crime, Lupe was undaunted. This would not have happened in the first place, she maintained, had they not been so poor, and after all, their poverty was essentially the fault of the rich. Tulcaneses thus believe that they are completely at the mercy of those with more resources.

The poor also resent the patronizing and condescending attitude which they believe the wealthy have toward them. One day when talking about the problems of being poor, Faustina de Arias said, "The rich say we poor spend all our money on soda pop. But, I ask you, where do we get the wherewithal to pay for these soft drinks?" No, she continued, the poor are not poor because they have frivolous spending habits or because they are not able to save what little they earn. They are poor because they are not permitted to live any other way. Tulcaneses harbor no doubts that they are just as capable as the oligarchy and many feel that, given the chance, they could run the country in a better, more equitable manner than does, as Héctor Arias puts it, "the rotating oligarchy which does nothing but eat, fornicate, and sleep while the people slave to support them." I heard this statement, with variations, many times.

Yet in spite of their vitriolic denunciations of the oligarchy as a whole, Tulcaneses speak fondly of members of this group whom they know personally. The man who subdivided the land on which the barrio is built is always referred to in the most complimentary and glowing terms. Several medical doctors and dentists are also praised for their skills and humanitarian concerns. Tulcanés women sometimes describe particular upper-class women they know as "magnificent people," as do their husbands in talking about men of the oligarchy for whom they have worked. It is almost as if they are saying: "Oligarchs are exploitative people, and we would be very much better off without them. Nevertheless, I have never met one whom I did not like and admire."

Although Tulcaneses believe that an unscrupulous oligarchy takes advantage of them at every turn, they can see ways in which their situation might improve, even though they admit that their plans may never be realized. Luck—coupled with divine intervention—is seen to be the most important possibility for improving their situation. As one resident rather philosophically observed, "God helps you or he doesn't." Praying to the right saints, Tulcaneses note, also helps.

Education is another way in which Tulcaneses feel they can get ahead, for they realize that many jobs require at least an elementary knowledge of reading and arithmetic. Whether they are candidates for positions in large stores or as night watchmen, they usually end up taking tests, the primary aim of which is to reduce the number of contenders by eliminating the less educated.

Many Tulcaneses see change coming through political processes. For some, the belief in the inevitability of a revolution in the near future permits them to remain patient a while longer, while others feel that peaceful political and social evolution will advance their cause.

Tulcaneses see themselves as a unit vis-à-vis the outside world, and they all claim membership in the lower class, but no one seriously would claim that everyone is equal within the barrio. Speaking for many, Jaime Torres notes, "We are not all equal, naturally, but we are all poor." Rather than speaking of "richer" and "poorer" when conversing about themselves and their neighbors, Tulcaneses talk in euphemistic terms. Hernán Granada stated, "Some say we are equal, that we all suffer the same. That isn't true. I, for example, suffer less than my neighbor here, but I suffer more than others. They have an easier life." Or, says another, "Some individuals in the barrio have better 'proportions' than others." Still others speak of some people in the barrio as being "better adapted" than others.

I asked Adolfo Samboni if the barrio has people living in it other than those from the lower class. No, he replied, the first thing someone with enough money to be considered other than lower-class would do would be to move to another neighborhood. There are no lawyers, bank tellers, medical doctors, or engineers in the barrio. Still, barrio residents agree that those of their numbers who are the most "comfortable" have steady, salaried jobs, preferably with the local or departmental government.

When I asked friends to name the five richest families in the barrio, there was very little consensus; they had trouble deciding who the wealthiest in the barrio were. Further, in spite of the salaried, steadily employed people being considered the "most comfortable," the Tulcaneses generally named as the richest were families in which the household head worked in construction or owned a store in the barrio. Proximity also played an important role, for people tended to name individuals or families who lived close to them. Perhaps the lack of consensus may be explained by the simple fact that movement in and out of the barrio, plus a lack of any real community cohesiveness, prevent inhabitants from getting to know each other well, and contacts often are limited to immediate neighbors. Also, in asking people to list the wealthiest residents in the barrio, I was asking them to speculate on a subject to which they previously had not given much thought. In any case, no one named the families who were, according to my data, the wealthiest.

When asked who the five poorest were, most Tulcaneses would not even attempt a choice. They replied that there were so many needy people in the barrio that they had no idea who were the poorest. Those who did list fellow residents almost inevitably included themselves. When I inquired among the others who did not list themselves among the poorest families if they considered themselves to be among the richest or the poorest, the general reply was among the poorest, even if it should have been clear to them this was not the case.

SOCIAL INTERACTION

In spite of professed pride in Tulcán, there is very little community cohesiveness, and the desire of inhabitants to remain aloof from social entanglements is evident in several ways. For instance, residents say that they have few good friends living in the barrio, and they know the names of very few of their neighbors, calling them "neighbor" or "fellow-countryman." Tulcaneses always address one another as *usted* (the formal Spanish "you"), and insist on calling each other by the formal, respectful *don* for men and *doña* (or its equivalent, *mísia*) for women before their given names, even if they have known each other for years.

When Tulcaneses meet on the street, greetings are short, verging on being curt; men rarely shake hands and women do not embrace. They do not inquire about members of each other's families, perhaps not wanting to get involved even at that level. In comparison, whenever higher-class Payanés friends meet, they shake hands and exchange embraces, even if they have seen each other recently. And when Tulcaneses interact with people of a higher social class, they too shake hands and are very genteel and cordial, exhibiting a type of behavior not demonstrated among lower-class social equals.

Tulcaneses remain aloof even in their drinking behavior, for drinking is usually a solitary experience. In the barrio's cantinas, men sit by themselves, listening to music and sipping their beers or staring at their shot glasses of aguardiente. No social pressures are placed on drinking and, in fact, excessive drinking is not widespread and spending money on intoxicants is frowned upon. Yet, on certain occasions men do drink together. Weddings, baptisms, certain religious holidays, and the arrival of a friend or relative from the countryside result in the consumption of copious quantities of *guarapo* (fermented sugarcane juice), beer, and aguardiente. In these instances, residents may invite neighbors or a few kinsmen to celebrate with them.

There are virtually no barrio-wide associations in Tulcán. While the Junta is set up as such, its leaders receive little cooperation from barrio residents, and at present not much benefit is derived from it. The organizations which are supposed to govern the school and build the barrio chapel consist in large part of the same individuals who are leaders in the Junta, and neither group is very effective, nor do they receive much community support. There are no mutual aid societies in the barrio, and voluntary associations are limited to a barrio soccer team and to a group of men who compete for Tulcán in the city tejo championships.

At the same time, on an individual basis, Tulcaneses can be quite generous and helpful. While Jaime Saturino never participates in community work projects, he willingly helped his neighbor, Jaime Torres, to remove tree stumps from his back yard. Tulcaneses will take in homeless old people who can no longer make a living, and many make small, periodic financial contributions to church charities or give a few centavos to beggars. They are sympathetic to the plight of others and, if asked, will give vegetables from their gardens or rice or a few sticks of wood to a neighbor in need.

In spite of their desire to live independently, assistance is occasionally necessary in every family, and Tulcaneses periodically are obliged to call on friends and neighbors for aid. Most Tulcaneses have loose-knit networks of individuals with whom they exchange gifts and on whom they can rely in times of need (cf. Wolf 1966; Mitchell 1969). In discussing dyadic contracts in Tzintzuntzan, Mexico, Foster states, "A very important functional requirement of the system is that *an exactly even balance between two partners never be struck.* This would jeopardize the whole relationship since, if all credits and debits somehow could be balanced off at one time, the contract would cease to exist" (1967:219).

In Tulcán, just the opposite is true: a gift or favor by Party A is repaid by Party B as quickly as possible. In this way, the individual satisfies his need and at the same time remains free of entanglements by repaying his benefactor within a very short time. The system functions because of the ease and availability with which such contracts can be established. For example, one morning I was watching Jaime Torres make a window frame when Carmen de Aguirre came in with vegetables for Jaime's wife, Victoria. Half an hour later, Carmen left, taking with her the empty vegetable basket and a bowl of fresh sancocho covered neatly with a cloth napkin. The gift was given and repaid within that short time, and while the families were building a tradition of exchanging with each other, each remained free of obligations to the other.

In some instances, the flow of exchanges between families is almost continuous. For example, one neighbor uses the water of another on a regular basis to wash his clothes, repaying his friend each time by bringing over some scraps for the family dog. Perhaps Faustina de Arias expressed the concept best when a neighbor boy came over with a large pan filled with vegetable scraps for Jaime and Faustina's pig. After Faustina had emptied the pan into a nearby pail, she gave Juan a handful of sticks from the woodpile. "It was a gift," she told me, "but you have to give something in return so they do not forget you."

CONFLICT RESOLUTION
Tulcaneses feel that it is desirable to avoid any form of direct physical or verbal confrontations which might result in a loss of temper or face for someone; thus, the person who fights

FIGURE 4. Neighbors enjoying a late-afternoon break. Note treadle sewing machine, which has been moved outside so its operator can work and socialize at the same time.

(physically) or argues is considered undesirable. People go out of their way to avoid conflicts even if it means not rectifying a situation that is unjust. Darío Ramos was very pleased when a municipal "fence inspector" arrived in the barrio one day to check for property line transgressions. Tulcán's roads are very crooked, and in most cases, anyone moving his fence out a yard or two would go unnoticed; but Darío was distressed at the number of violations he knew about, and he wanted action. The Junta, he noted, would not consider the issue and he could not directly intervene himself because he did not want a confrontation.

The desire to avoid verbal confrontations appears in speech. Tulcaneses often preface remarks with "as the saying goes," even when it is obvious the speaker is not repeating a common saying or belief but is expressing his own opinion. By stating the opinion as a general belief, he avoids the possibility that the person to whom he is speaking will disagree and ask him to defend his statement. When talking about future action they plan to take, Tulcaneses are likely to say, "if God wills it" or "if the Virgin permits." The speaker thus acknowledges the possibility that he might not take the action in the end and, in that case, wishes to remain blameless.

At times, disputes occur which cannot be avoided, and then it is up to the parties involved to work out a satisfactory settlement among themselves. Perhaps the difficulties inherent in such action emphasize the reasons for avoiding conflicts in the first place, for in Tulcán, there are neither traditions nor mechanisms for handling disputes. Nor is there an outside agency which can aid them in conflict resolution: the Junta has no powers to settle disputes and Tulcaneses look upon the courts and the judicial process as not designed to help them.

The general rule for resolving disputes is simply to reestablish the status quo. For example, after drinking guarapo all night, José López broke an empty bottle over Pedro Alemán's head, and Pedro had to have twelve stitches taken in his head and face. The neighbors agreed that José's actions were very "antisocial" and eventually, without legal sanction, José agreed to pay the hospital bill and the equivalent of two days of work for the time Pedro was unable to operate as a hauler.

ENVY AND GOSSIP

Because of the limited number of jobs available to unskilled workers in Popayán, many Tulcaneses tend to look upon their environment as fixed or closed, offering them few opportunities for immediate change (cf. Foster 1965, 1971).[3] The limited economic possibilities in turn restrict options in other areas, and people without some financial resources find it difficult to obtain reasonable health care or education for their children. There is a great deal of competition for the few opportunities which do exist, and each person worries that his neighbors will get ahead at his expense, perhaps taking a job with the municipal government which he had applied for a few days earlier. There is also resentment toward those who, for no apparent reason, manage to get ahead. Samuel Méndez notes that if someone in the barrio has good fortune, other barrio residents will stop greeting him in the streets, and after a while, they will start talking behind his back, saying that he did not deserve such good luck and that he is no good. Manuel Calderón echoes this feeling: "Referring to myself, I know that my neighbors are envious of me. They see this house. It is not

3. In describing the "Image of Limited Good" Foster states, "I mean that broad areas of peasant behavior are patterned in such fashion as to suggest that peasants view their social, economic, and natural universes—their total environment—as one in which all of the desired things in life such as land, wealth, health, friendship and love, manliness and honor, respect and status, power and influence, security and safety, *exist in finite quantity* and *are always in short supply*, as far as the peasant is concerned" (1965:296). A corollary to the Image of Limited Good is: "if 'Good' exists in limited amounts which cannot be expanded, and if the system is closed, it *follows that an individual or a family can improve a position only at the expense of others*" (1965:296–97). As Foster points out (1965:311, and 1971:3), numerous aspects of this cognitive model are by no means exclusive of peasant behavior. Barrio Tulcán is certainly not a "closed" society; but, importantly, its inhabitants look at "good" opportunities as preciously few in number—and definitely not enough for all. Attitudes toward someone who lands a well-paying, secure job are not characterized by felicitations and best wishes for being fortunate, but rather by a feeling that "the job should have been mine and he got it at my expense." Thus, I have found some parts of this model helpful in explaining and interpreting actions and attitudes of urban Tulcaneses.

In contrast, in her study of social mobility and industrialization in Uzice, Yugoslavia, Denitch states that residents operate according to an "image of unlimited good" (1969:144). Rather than seeing their environment as limited and fixed, the Uziacani, who live in a rapidly industrializing area in a socialist country, see themselves with essentially unlimited opportunities for improvement.

very elegant, but it is large. They say, 'How can a poor man who sells sweets for a living have a house that large?' I know there are rumors about me. They probably think I sleep by day and work by night as a thief. If you work hard and better yourself, people will think you are a thief, or they will say you have found a pot of treasure. Everybody has heard stories about people making pacts with the devil in the mountains over there and getting rich that way."

The fear of envy does not keep people from trying to get ahead, but they hope to avoid envy in other ways. When Tulcaneses entertain guests, the normally shuttered windows are opened and neighbors are free to drop by for a bite to eat and a small glass of rum or aguardiente. When anyone gets something new, he explains that it is the property of anyone who desires it. When I commented on David Narváez's new horse, he replied, "I got it last week and it is yours"— symbolically saying, "Do not be envious of me because I have something you do not have. I offer it to you."

Tulcaneses seek to control the actions of their neighbors through gossip. When someone allows the facade of his house to fall into disrepair, his neighbors will not confront him directly with their dissatisfaction about this, but will gossip about him. Manuel Calderón feels that gossip is endemic to the poor. "You cannot do anything without having everyone comment," he says. "If you have a drink, or see a woman, maybe dance a little, people tell your wife. We lower-class people talk too much. It is impossible to enjoy yourself without someone telling your wife, 'Oh, your husband was drinking.'"

It is through gossip that Tulcaneses attempt to impose the stronger social sanction of ostracism. In a barrio with so much anonymity, this is effective only in sections where people have known each other long enough to exchange gossip and to be upset when it is directed at them. After leaving her common-law husband, María Molina was forced out of the house into which she had moved because of rumors and gossip about her loose behavior, and she went to live with her half-sister on the other side of the barrio where she was unknown. Eventually she mended her ways and came back to live with Pedro, but she continued to be a social outcast among the women in that section of the barrio.

Although gossip usually has a derogatory effect, it is perhaps the only effective means available to Tulcaneses to keep a modicum of social order in their world.

EXPECTATIONS: THE IDEAL PERSON

After many conversations with residents, a picture emerges of how the ideal Tulcanés behaves. Within the family, the most important quality of the adult is a sense of responsibility toward his dependents; he must care for his offspring by feeding and dressing them properly, educating them, and making them respectful. A man who drinks while his children go hungry or a woman who neglects her brood is deemed irresponsible. At the same time, children reflect on their parents, and people talk if they do not contribute actively to the betterment of the household by working and studying, or if they go undisciplined and have no manners.

Working hard is a virtue, and although some men work only half-days and appear to relax the rest of the time, holding down a job or working to support the family in one way or another is highly important. In an area where so little work is available and so much un- and underemployment prevails, there seems to be surprisingly little sympathy for those individuals who cannot find work of some kind or who allow members of the family who are potential breadwinners to remain idle. Once I mentioned to Miguel Agredo that I had talked with many people who were unable to find work. He answered angrily that those who said things like that just did not want to work. He maintained that there was work to be had if the individual really wanted it, but too many people put forth their own specifications for jobs and would not accept what was available. When Lupe Martínez asked Jaime Arias to help her two teen-age sons find jobs, he offered to take them with him to cut firewood, for which there is a considerable market in the barrio. The boys went twice and then stopped going. Jaime concluded that they were being irresponsible because they were not making use of an opportunity to earn money and that Lupe also was to blame for permitting her sons to behave in this way.

Finally, the ideal Tulcanés should be *formal* (reliable), not *vulgar* (coarse or common), and not *egoista* (selfish). A selfish person invites envy—something to be avoided at all costs.

6. The Family

O F THE 275 barrio households, the nuclear family—a married
or unmarried couple with or without children—is the ideal
and most prevalent (53 per cent) form.[1] However, due to the
high number of free unions, strict bilaterality is not common
among Tulcaneses. Truncated families—those with an absent
father or mother—account for 12 per cent of these households;
nearly three-quarters of these are headed by women, most of
whom are unmarried, but some of whom are widowed or
abandoned. The remainder are extended families (21 per

1. In his study of a suburb of Oaxaca, Mexico, Chance notes that his
original analysis indicated a high incidence of nuclear family household types,
but when the data were reorganized with the concept of "extended family enclaves" included, this contention was greatly modified. "Once household and
family are clearly distinguished, the incidence of the nuclear family as a
kinship unit is seen to be relatively low, since many units which are commonly classified as families are in fact components of larger extended family
groupings which may include three or more (usually nuclear) households"
(Chance 1971:133). In Tulcán there was no evidence of contiguous family
households which could be regarded as "extended family enclaves": families
either lived together in the same household and were classified as extended
families, or were scattered throughout the barrio, separated by considerable
distance.

cent)—those with married children and perhaps grand-children—and households composed of two unrelated nuclear families, or parts of families, living together (14 per cent). Regardless of the type of household composition, the family's function is to give its members at least minimal economic and emotional securities and educational opportunities, as well as to provide a sexual and reproductive outlet.

COURTSHIP AND MARRIAGE

For barrio youngsters, interest in the opposite sex and accompanying courtship patterns differ little in many respects from those of their peers in other societies. Teen-age girls spend hours reading and exchanging *foto-novelas* (love-story comic books with photographs instead of drawings) or sit transfixed listening to romantic radio soap operas. Young men stand around barrio stores, talking about the good-looking girls in Tulcán and neighboring barrios. The finely turned leg of a barrio beauty brings comments, wolf whistles, and appreciative gazes.

Dating among teenagers, however, is not common. Parents discourage it, for they try to exercise a watchful eye over their daughters, while financial limitations all but preclude taking a girl and a chaperon to a movie. Instead, socializing is done in large groups as teen-agers of both sexes walk together through the barrio streets or stand in front of one of the stores, chatting and laughing. When a boy becomes more serious about a girl, he goes to her house and calls on her parents, asking them if he may visit their daughter there. If the parents approve, the young couple then may talk together in the yard of the girl's house or in the street in front. Should the parents disapprove, the couple either must call off the budding courtship or meet clandestinely. If a secret relationship were discovered, the girl would be punished by her father, and the boy would risk a physical confrontation with the girl's father or brothers.

In spite of these theoretical courtship restrictions, and the supposedly protective measures instituted by fathers and brothers to guard the virginity of their women, it is common for teen-age girls to have children out of wedlock. When this happens, the girl and child frequently remain at home, the child becomes practically a sibling to its uncles and aunts (who eventually may bracket it in age), and the incident is considered closed. Generally, however, prolonged courtship leads to marriage.

Marriage follows one of two routes. Most common is elopement, called *robo* (robbery), in which the pair runs away for a couple of days, perhaps staying with friends of the boy who live in another part of town or in a village outside of Popayán. When a girl is "robbed," fathers and brothers become angry because their family's honor has been besmirched, but in Tulcán (unlike many Latin American peasant villages described in anthropological literature) this does not necessarily mean a wedding is in the offing. The girl's parents, in fact, have four alternatives: the girl may be brought back, reprimanded for her loose ways, and kept at home; the girl's father may go to the police, press charges of kidnapping against the young man, and have him jailed; the couple may set up housekeeping and live together in free union; the couple may marry.

The alternative way of getting married begins with the boy formally asking the girl's parents for her hand. Once the marriage has been approved, the couple then has time to buy items they will need to set up housekeeping and to make arrangements for the wedding with the priest. Most Tulcanés weddings are held on Saturday in the chapel of the Barrio Alfonso López; generally, they are group marriages which include any other couples in the parish who wish to get married on that particular Saturday. Following the ceremony, the couple returns to the house of one of the families, and dinner is served to relatives and special guests. After this, dancing and drinking begin which last through the night, and perhaps through the following day.

Héctor Arias chose the second method of getting married. For him, the decision to marry his girlfriend of several years came after he took over Enrique Aguirre's job salting skins and got a house in the barrio. He told me, "It happened that I have had various sweethearts and all that. But when they talked of getting married, it seemed impossible. Getting married, well, it really happened from one moment to the next. I talked to her about it and she could not believe me. When I told her my idea about getting married, she said, 'Well, whatever you think.' When the time came, I told her to go get her baptismal certificate. It was not something we had thought about for very long. It was really a question of, well, I got this job and I thought, 'What am I going to do living here by myself?' I needed someone, so I did this thing." Since Elena's father had died a few years before, Héctor asked her brother for permission to marry her.

In Barrio Tulcán free unions are very common. Tulcaneses claim that to a certain extent free unions are an urban phenomenon, and in fact, couples that come in from the country together almost always are married. On the other hand, migrants who are single when they arrive in Popayán show just as high a tendency to enter into free-union relationships as do Tulcaneses who were born in Popayán or have come from other urban areas.

There are a number of reasons why free unions occur in Tulcán more frequently than in rural areas. The general economic instability of Popayán makes them an attractive alternative for some men because if they get into financial difficulty, they are able to leave their spouses without fear of legal action.[2] Again, because divorces are unobtainable in Colombia, free unions are the only alternative for individuals whose civil and religious marriages have not worked out. Partners in free unions justify their relationship by saying it is more honest than marriage. Because they are not married, they say, they are free to come and go as they please. Thus, in a free union it is not necessary to cheat on one's spouse. Further, the couple stays together because they want to, not because they feel obligated to.

Samuel Méndez, currently living with his second common-law wife, feels this arrangement is healthy for him as well as for Elodia. The children from such unions have all the legal rights of those born to married couples and, Samuel says, the only circumstances under which he would marry Elodia would be if either of them were about to die. This, he feels, would take care of the sin of living together in an unmarried state and would assure the dying member entrance into heaven (although he is unsure if he believes in it).

2. In recent years Colombian law has changed, making desertion, even in cases of free-union couples, punishable by fines and imprisonment; but most Tulcaneses do not know about these laws. Furthermore, because they fear that nothing would come of it except financial expense, women are reluctant to press charges.

Tulcaneses note that although free unions do occur in the countryside, they are not nearly as common as in the urban setting. In isolated areas, a couple may live in free union for a year or so before getting married, but generally they succumb to pressures from the visiting priest, who often will perform group marriages for all couples in the immediate area who have not been married since his previous visit. Tulcaneses feel that in rural areas, people are much more likely to believe the priest when he tells them that if they are living in sin, they will not go to heaven when they die. Pressures are placed on the unmarried couple by friends and relatives who maintain that the married state is the only way for a couple to live. In the city, and even in a quasi-village situation like Barrio Tulcán, there is enough anonymity to permit free unions to take place and pregnant girls to remain unmarried without the individuals bowing to external pressures.

ROLES IN THE FAMILY

By all appearances, the father is the unquestioned head of the family in the ideal Tulcanés household: he is able to do as he pleases, and he is accountable only to himself for his actions. If he wants to cheat on his wife, he may, and few will question the double standard which never permits a married woman to do the same thing. These attitudes were clear from discussions and also from Thematic Apperception Tests. One picture shows "A woman is clutching the shoulders of a man whose face and body are averted as if he were trying to pull away from her" (Murray 1943:19). While the reactions of Tulcaneses varied from such statements as "The man is drunk and his wife is helping him" to "The man is abandoning his wife," the most common response was that the wife has found out her husband has a mistress and is asking him to leave her and come home. María Cruz said, "I think that in the life of this man there must be another person, no? Another, another wife or some other woman in the life of this man. For this reason, he no longer loves his wife, his real one. And she wants him to forget the other woman and to return to her, and I think that she is suffering a great deal, and he is smiling." However, María went on to say that in the end, he would return to his wife. Micaela de Miranda, looking at the picture, expressed the opinion that the wife is angry at her husband because he has other women and that in the end the man will go with his mistress.

The role of the mother in the household is simply stated: she is to be hardworking and obedient to her spouse. There is no ambiguity in the division of labor. The mother is responsible for keeping the house clean and organized, for doing the shopping, and for cooking the meals. The father does not interfere in these matters, just as she would not question him in his activities. Yet, in reality, the wife has considerable voice in family affairs, particularly in the socialization of the children and in most monetary matters.

From the age of four or five, children are expected to assume considerable responsibility; they are called upon to perform a variety of tasks, and playing takes place only after all work is done. Primarily, children help their mothers with household chores and go to stores in the barrio throughout the day to pick up necessary items. When five-year-old Jesús Valencia was shortchanged at one of the barrio stores, his mother was furious with him. She berated him severely for being foolish and sent him back to the store where, weeping, he pleaded his case with the store owner. To the store owner, this had been a game; confronted with cheating, she quickly and good-humoredly returned the few centavos owed him.

Children also care for younger siblings. Miguelangel Peña, also five, takes care of his three-year-old sister and three-week-old baby brother while his mother works in the barrio school cafeteria. In addition, older male children become surrogate fathers and are supposed to watch over their sisters. When eighteen-year-old José Cruz caught his thirteen- and fifteen-year-old sisters talking with a couple of boys, he slapped them around and practically dragged them home by their hair. His actions met with parental approval and the girls were punished for their "loose" behavior.

As children grow older, they are expected to attend school, get a job, or, if they are female, to work at home on a full-time basis. Families become very distressed when teen-age sons are not productive; this leads to gossip and criticism from neighbors who, on most other issues, do not care one way or another what a family does. The reason for this attitude is that most families can hardly wait until the children are old enough to help support the family. When these people see unproductive

FIGURE 5. View of Barrio Tulcán's main street.

teen-agers, they regard them as bad examples for their children. When Nemecio Gómez was unable to get work, his neighbor, Micaela de Miranda, commented to me that it was too bad that his fifteen-year-old son did not find some way of bringing in money to help the family, and she finally concluded that the father was good but the son was worthless: "The fingers on the hand are not the same."

EDUCATION

Parents who can afford it send their children to school, since most look upon education as a primary means of improving their position in life. This is apparent not only from the many conversations and interviews I had, but also from Thematic Apperception Tests in which residents told stories about children who become successful through diligent study and hard work. The following, selected for their clarity, are typical examples of such stories:

Card 1. "A young boy is contemplating a violin which rests on a table in front of him" (Murray 1943:18).
   Respondent (an eighteen-year-old female): "The boy is thinking. In the future he will continue studying. Then he will help his parents. In reality, because his family is so poor, he will help them a great deal."
   Respondent (a twenty-one-year-old male): "This is a boy who is studying a musical instrument. He is thinking about learning to play it. Later he will become a great musician and will earn many pesos."

Card 2. "Country Scene: in the foreground is a young woman with books in her hand; in the background a man is working the fields and an older woman is looking on" (Murray 1943:18).
   Respondent (a forty-five-year-old male): "There is a man with a horse. He is looking and possibly thinking that this horse is going to plow many more furrows. We also see a woman or girl looking at a statue. She has books in her hand. These books probably will bring her much knowledge in the future. She will learn to live better from them. But she is very pensive and is very sad. She must be very happy to think that

with time, they will help her to be a great person, a wise person. The person who knows how to study is the most capable to earn the best salaries in whatever country. She is probably a little sad because in order to do this, she is going to have a hard time. But with time, it will be all right."

Respondent (a twenty-one-year-old male): "She is looking at the field and looking at the horse that transports the produce. She realizes that manual labor is difficult. Therefore, it is better to study in order to have an easier life. That is the conclusion I find here."

Card 16. Blank; the individual asked to make up story.

Respondent (a forty-one-year-old female): "This card represents some children in a school. The children are playing in an old tire. One of the children trips and falls, hurting his foot. They have to take him to the hospital, but the parents do not have any money. They must go and get a loan in order to pay for the child's cast. The child gets better, studies hard, and finishes school. He then becomes a great artist and helps his parents a great deal because they have sacrificed so much for him."

Thus, Tulcaneses regard education as enabling people to better "defend" themselves: it is the key to breaking out from engulfing impoverishment and consequently plays an extremely important role in the lives of many families. They see that people with money and good jobs also know how to read and write and conclude that there must be some relationship between the two. Widow Andrea de Arenas says that her life goal is to educate her children "so they will not have to suffer like I have." Some families felt so strongly about the need to educate their children that they moved in from the country at considerable financial sacrifice because a good education is available only in the city.

In fact, some education is essential for getting most steady jobs. As we have seen, applicants for work in practically any small industry or establishment are given tests covering Colombia's history, geography, and political system, and mathematics. Often these tests have no bearing on the job, but are used purely for eliminating candidates. Even if the family believes there is nothing to be gained from schooling, there is pressure from neighbors and priests to send children to classes. School gets children out from underfoot and eliminates the necessity for adult supervision by a family member who might otherwise be working. Children at the barrio school are assured of one good meal a day, since CARE provides them with staples for a hot lunch. Finally, Tulcaneses feel that education, like eating and sleeping, has something intrinsically good about it, although they are not sure exactly what that is. Education, says Jesús Díaz, is a "civilizing" factor which presents his children with an urban world view.

It is not always easy for parents to convince school-age members of the family that education has its virtues, in spite of their enthusiasm. Many children claim that education leads nowhere and that classes are not stimulating, challenging, or even interesting. Indeed, the rote memorization that forms the basis for learning tends to stifle incentive, and students often become discouraged and quit.

Perhaps one reason children are unenthusiastic about school is the lack of an educational atmosphere at home. Few homes have any kind of reading material, except for an occasional newspaper or comic book, and consequently it is difficult for children to become motivated academically. Jorge and Marta Cruz firmly believe in the necessity of getting a good education as a means of getting ahead in the world. They have tried to instill this belief in their children and were extremely upset when their first three children dropped out of school after the fourth grade. Yet the only literature in the house consists of Jorge's comic books, and the Cruz children do not need more than a fourth-grade education to emulate their father. When I asked fifteen-year-old María Cruz why she had failed fourth grade, she replied, "Well, I suppose I spent too much time in school reading comic books when I should have been studying."

When people decide to send their children to school or to attend classes themselves, they can choose one of several schools. Next to the health center in the barrio is Tulcán's public school, which, like many rural schools, has only three grades. In the late afternoon, there is an adult school run by nuns and senior high school girls from Colegio San José de Tarbas in Popayán. Initially, there was considerable enthusiasm about these classes; now many candidly admit they go principally for credit slips which can be exchanged for food and clothing.

Even though it is an additional expense, many families prefer to send their children to private lower-class schools in Popayán because they are convinced that the children receive a better education there. There are also two night schools in the Barrio Alfonso López which draw students from Tulcán, and some parents and children attend classes there together. Various trade and technical schools are open to residents, and a number of Tulcaneses have studied such diverse subjects as accounting, sewing, typing, cattle raising, and the handling and maintenance of farm machinery. Acción Católica teaches crocheting, the Red Cross instructs in hygiene, and the Colegio Normal Superior de Señoritas conducts classes in sewing.

For most barrio families, real education is an unattainable dream. It is poverty more than a lack of desire that prevents many Tulcaneses from sending their children to school, for even in the public schools, books and supplies must be purchased by the student. Furthermore, after children reach the age of ten or eleven, they become potential breadwinners, and parents must decide whether continued education or additional income is more important. While most barrio children attend school at some time during their lives, few get past the fifth grade, and there are no high-school graduates in Tulcán.

FAMILY RELATIONSHIPS

It is obvious that parents often derive undisguised happiness from their children. Mothers carry children around, kiss them, and comfort them when they fall or are being harassed by an older sibling. Fathers, too, hug their little ones, bear them on their shoulders, and in general seem very pleased to have them. When parents meet children after an absence of a couple of hours, or when children are about to leave, parents always stop what they are doing to bless the children by making the sign of the cross over the child's forehead and saying, "May God watch over you."

Except for major infractions of rules, the job of disciplining children falls to the mother, and while some women are very concerned that their children be polite and act "correctly," others do not seem to care how their children behave. I never saw a child spanked; rather, punishment consisted of such things as restriction to the house, denial of food, or a threat to give a misbehaving child to the "crazy woman," the equivalent of a bogeyman.

Married couples demonstrate none of the overt affection that they shower so openly upon their children. Public physical contact is unheard of, as are affectionate names or any other display of warmth. A man may show that he cares for a woman by occasionally beating her, and although too much of this "affection" may lead to the dissolution of the household, women expect some of it and feel that it indicates they are not being taken for granted. Once, after telling María Santos that I did not beat my wife, she asked in an astonished tone, "Why, how do you show Patricia that you love her?"

Birth control among Tulcaneses appears to be unknown, although it is felt that nursing prevents pregnancy. If barrio residents do know about methods for controlling conception, it is a well-kept secret. The usual response to the question "What is the ideal number of children a couple should have?" was "All that God sends." Still, Tulcaneses believe that it is desirable to have larger families in the countryside because the additional labor is needed, while in the city the family should be smaller because it is more expensive to feed, clothe, and educate children. The local health clinic does not dispense information on family planning, and although the Red Cross once showed a movie in the community center on the importance of limiting the number of children, people are at a loss as to how to obtain birth control information.

In general, family ties in Tulcán are not strong, particularly those of the extended family, and in many respects the role of friends is as important as that of kinsmen.[3] There are at least three reasons for this. First, the prevalence of free unions tends to keep strong family networks from developing. Although some free unions are stable, the majority last only a few years—long enough, perhaps, for the pair to have a couple of children—before the adults go their separate ways. In a number of free-union households, each adult brings children from previous unions into the home. In these cases, each adult is responsible for the actions of his or her children. Samuel

3. Havens and Flinn note the importance of the role of the extended family, particularly in the maintenance of social power, in Barrio Tolima, an illegal subdivision on the outskirts of Bogotá (1970a:103).

Méndez has two boys from a previous free union, and his common-law wife, Elodia Arroyo, has one son, the same age as Samuel's oldest. Elodia allows her offspring to go into town, and while Samuel disapproves of this and does not permit his sons to do the same, he does not question Elodia's authority over her son. Sometimes full siblings from free unions are separated when some accompany the man and others go with the woman when the partners dissolve their union. In these situations, it is difficult for strong ties to develop, and little emphasis or importance is placed on them.

Second, the process of migration may reduce interaction and communication between members of a family; after a while the ties atrophy, and eventually contacts may cease altogether. However—although this is not often the case—family contacts also may be renewed and strengthened through migration, so the process may be a two-way street.

Third, poverty may prevent strong ties from developing among members of a family. Part of being able to "defend" oneself is to live without crippling obligations to members of extended families. Extended families are most prevalent among the poorest and most affluent people, the poorest because they must stick together to survive, and the most affluent because they can afford to permit other members of their family to live with them. But people in the middle, who are well off enough to be fairly independent, discourage family ties which can and do drain their limited resources. Their strategy is to tap the aid of kinsmen when in need of their assistance—such as when arriving in Popayán from the countryside and looking for a place to stay and a job—but to be able to shed them when they become a financial burden.

Naturally, there are exceptions to this: the very old and the very young often are found living with these "average" families. Nieces and nephews come in from the country and live with relatives while they attend school, and some aging parents move in with their children. In a number of cases, old people who are no longer breadwinners—and perhaps even complete strangers—practically are adopted by Tulcanés families. In one such incident, María Santos took in an elderly woman, noting simply that "The old one came here and asked if she could stay as she had no other place to go."

COMPADRAZGO

Compadrazgo (co-godparenthood) reciprocal relationships are established between individuals through participation in several Catholic rites—specifically, in Tulcán, when a child is baptized and confirmed. In addition, when a couple marries, they acquire wedding godparents, but unlike elsewhere in Latin America (e.g., Gillin 1947:105; Foster 1967:76; Service and Service 1965:13; Ravicz 1967:246–48), this is not considered important in the compadrazgo system. Ideally, the relationships which develop from compadrazgo—child and ceremonial sponsor, parents and sponsor—are sacred, involving mutual respect, and at least implying exchanges of food, drink, and help. Yet, this fictive kinship is not very important to most Tulcaneses, and while every child has godparents for the appropriate occasions, the attendant activities are not always observed.

Since Tulcán is a part of the parish of Alfonso López, baptisms are supposed to take place in the parish chapel. Sometimes, however, parents prefer the larger and more elegant churches of San Francisco or San Augustín in the center of town. To baptize a child in one or the other of these churches, parents simply give a false address which corresponds to the parish of the church they select. Baptisms, brief and lacking in fanfare, are held at two o'clock in the afternoon, with as many as ten or fifteen babies receiving the blessing simultaneously. Custom does not dictate any fiesta afterward, although if the families have been good friends before, the group may go from the church to the house of one of the participants, where aguardiente or a few bottles of beer will be consumed.

Most Tulcanés confirmations take place on the Día de la Asención del Señor (Feast of the Ascension), when there is a mass confirmation in the church in Alfonso López that includes children from other parts of the parish as well. After the major ceremony, the priest says a special mass for barrio participants in the community meeting hall, which is followed by small parties held in the houses of the parents whose children have been confirmed.

In most of Latin America, *compadres* (co-parents) give up the *tú* (familiar "you") form of address in favor of the more

respectful *usted* (formal "you"); in Tulcán, however, residents
address each other as usted at all times. As previously suggested, one of the reasons they do this is their desire to maintain social distance, thus avoiding friendship obligations and
entanglements. Furthermore, I would hypothesize that in
speaking to each other formally, Tulcaneses give one another a
type of respect which they, by virtue of their low social rank,
do not receive from people of higher classes. In any event, I
never heard adults—even married couples—address each other
in the familiar. As elsewhere in Latin America, after establishing compadrazgo ties, the couples involved address each other
as *compadre* or *compa* (co-father) and *comadre* (co-mother).

In Tulcán there is a striking dichotomy between real and
ideal modes of compadrazgo behavior (cf. Sayres 1956). Tulcaneses say that the compadrazgo is a very important and
sacred tie which unites compadres closer than brothers, and
entails seriousness, responsibility, and mutual respect. Similarly, appropriate rules of familial incest are recognized. A
slanderous statement would be, "Fulana is so despicable she
would live with her compadre," meaning the person in question has no more moral sense than a cat or a dog. When
Carmen Beltrán became the free-union spouse of the baptismal
godfather of her nine-year-old son, the incident was considered a sacrilege by her neighbors, and in Tulcán, everything said about her is prefaced by "She lives with her compadre." It was rumored that the two were almost run out of
Barrio Alfonso López because of their behavior.

The closeness which is supposed to develop from compadrazgo ties should be exemplified through frequent visits
between the two families and the periodic exchange of gifts
and favors. The relationship between the godparents
(*padrinos*) and the godchild (*ahijado*), too, should be one of
mutual respect, with the godchild being more eager to please
his godparents than his real ones and willing to help them at
any time. The godparents are supposed to play a vital role in
the spiritual development of the child, instructing him in religious and moral training, and if the child's natural parents
die, the baptismal godparents should become the adoptive
parents of their godchild.

In reality, things are far different. Many Tulcaneses cannot
remember the first or last names of the baptismal godparents of

their children. Casual acquaintances become compadres, and sometimes the sponsoring couple even asks to be the godparents of a child they like. After the ceremony, the couples may never again see each other. When questioned about visits and exchanging gifts, Tulcaneses admit that they perhaps should do it but do not—sometimes because they are not sure where their compadres are, but more often because they simply are uninterested in maintaining the tie.

Tulcaneses select compadres from two basic groups: kinsmen, with whom they have ready-made relationships by virtue of blood ties; and friends and acquaintances, some who are social and economic equals and others who are social and economic superiors. Social inferiors are never chosen. There seems to be no advantage in picking relatives, and it is not common practice; those selected are usually cousins, although Tulcaneses seemed surprised when I pointed this out, and maintained that there is no particular reason for it. Exceptional cases exist, such as that of Paco Díaz, who is the baptismal godfather of one of his grandchildren, something which occurred because Paco asked to sponsor the child.

There are, however, good reasons for picking social and economic equals as compadres. Horizontal contacts may cement an already strong friendship between two families, or they may confirm commercial ties. Tulcaneses view compadrazgo ties with social and economic superiors as a type of insurance (cf. Foster 1967:82–83). These vertical ties are useful, for example, if the family needs money for an emergency or, depending upon the occupation of the compadre, legal or medical services. Tulcaneses also realize that people in superior positions often like to acquire lower-class compadres because it makes them look charitable and concerned with the problems of the poor; sometimes such people even initiate the relationship by offering to serve as a child's godparents. Tulcaneses, for their part, patronize the stores of their rich compadres and recommend their services to friends and neighbors.

In addition, strangers are sometimes asked to be compadres. In one instance, Marco Gómez was standing in the church of San Augustín waiting for the rain to subside when a woman he had never seen before asked if he would be the baptismal godfather of her child, since the afternoon baptism was about to begin and the man she originally had asked had not appeared. Marco consented, went through the ceremony, and gave his comadre 10 pesos for the child before leaving. He does not remember their names and has not seen either since that day. Asking strangers to be compadres is not regarded as good practice, but it nevertheless happens with some frequency, emphasizing the unimportance of compadrazgo.

Although compadres traditionally are called upon in times of need, many Tulcaneses are relucant to ask for their help. When Rosa Arias was sick, I asked her mother, Faustina, why she did not take the girl to see her baptismal godfather, a pharmacist. To me this seemed like a natural thing to do, but while Faustina agreed in principle, she said, "One does not want to be shameful and bother the compadres," adding she "would rather starve before burdening compadres."

In fact, most Tulcaneses do not expect a great deal from their compadrazgo connections, either horizontal or vertical. At best they serve the ceremonial function of formalizing pre-existing friendship ties, but that is about all they do. More would violate the basic theme of living as independently as possible. The church requires compadres for baptism and confirmation, and this requirement is complied with, but no great effort is made to maintain the ties through such observances as visits and the exchange of gifts. In fact, families often seem to draw apart after the compadrazgo bond has been established, almost as if saying, "Let's not become too close and too mutually dependent." Thus, just as Tulcaneses play down the role of the family, so too is an effort made to de-emphasize the compadrazgo.

7. Political Institutions

The "Forgotten Ones"

MAN, IT IS SAID, is a political animal. This does not mean that everyone is an office seeker, but that at every level of life some form of politicking is found, and Tulcanés life is no exception to this rule. This chapter will discuss the political involvement of Tulcaneses at the barrio, municipal and departmental, and national levels: the political attitudes they hold, their activities, and the game plans they have for future political action.

BARRIO POLITICS AND ORGANIZATION

Tulcán is officially a barrio of Popayán and a semiautonomous neighborhood with its own elected council, legally known as the Pro-Barrio Junta de Acción Comunal, whose purpose is to organize the activities of the barrio, govern its actions, and act as its lobby to Popayán's mayor and Cauca's governor. This council is made up of representatives-at-large and delegates from *comités* (committees), the political divisions of the barrio.

The delegate from each committee is its "president," who is in theory responsible for watching over his section of the barrio. He is responsible for keeping the streets in his section free from grass and debris, as well as for periodically applying pressure on families to keep the facades of their houses neat. The head of each committee is also required to produce manpower from his section for the occasional *mingas* or *convites* (community work projects), although these are largely neglected both by the presidents of the committees and by the inhabitants. In reality, most people do not know or care who the head of their committee is. For all practical purposes, the committees are unworkable, and in 1971 the Junta was trying to abolish them.

Real power in the barrio is in the hands of the Junta president. Much like the mayor of a small town, he is the barrio's leader, and through him, the barrio voices its requests to the municipality and to the Department of Cauca. Also, like a small-town mayor, the Junta president receives a certain amount of prestige within the barrio, but he has practically no power outside it. Nevertheless, his job requires an enormous amount of energy, tenacity, free time, undying optimism, and the help of the municipal government in order to accomplish any of the barrio's needs and goals.

Shortly after I arrived in Popayán, Tulcaneses employed a new tactic in an effort to circumvent what they felt were the municipal power structure's attempts to ignore them. They elected as president a gentleman farmer, around whose hilltop the barrio has grown. Because he was head of a departmental agency in Popayán, Tulcaneses believed he had an automatic "in" with the government. Unfortunately, he was too busy managing his own affairs to exercise his potential power on the barrio's behalf, and he retired three months after he was elected without ever having attended a Junta meeting.

Regrettably, the Junta is largely ineffectual; its periodic meetings, held in the community hall and open to all barrio residents, mainly are occasions for the dissemination of information, in which the executive council informs those interested of what it is trying to do. The meetings do not serve as forums for debate; rather, issues are discussed in broad, general terms. People never really state opinions or take positions, and specific conclusions are not reached, other than the election of Junta officers.

Moreover, there is a general reluctance to get involved in the activities of the Junta, as well as those of the barrio. Some inhabitants go so far as to state that the Junta's activities infringe on their personal freedoms. Junta activities require at least tacit cooperation, be they tending the till at a fiesta held in the community center to raise money or working to install a couple of electric-light poles, and they can be time-consuming. Further, they may place one in the position of not only disagreeing with one's neighbor, but also forcing possible confrontations—something no one desires. Although verbally they take a good deal of pride in their barrio, Tulcaneses are disinclined to assist in projects for its good. The threat of being denied Junta assistance—such as the minga digging the connection from the sewer to an individual's house or, in a remote instance, granting a loan—is quite meaningless in coercing cooperation.

A major reason for the Junta's ineffectual status is that it does not intervene in disputes between barrio residents; it has no legal powers to do so, and the president feels that such intervention would probably undermine the Junta's power instead of increasing it. Consequently, the Junta president refrains from involvement in intra-barrio conflicts. Because social sanctions which might be used as controlling or leveling mechanisms (such as gossip, witchcraft, or social ostracism) are largely ineffective due to the anonymity and mobility of much of the barrio population, social or legal redress must come from the municipal authorities of Popayán itself.

Thus, although in theory the barrio government is well-organized, in practice it is quite powerless both in dealing with barrio affairs and, as will be shown, in obtaining services from the municipal government. Referring to the inability of the Junta to organize a minga to assist in a barrio clean-up after the nearby streams flooded, Jaime Saturino remarked, "The Junta is just like the fire department. They come when it is all over."

There is, however, a small group of families—all of whom have been living in the barrio for at least two years and most since its founding—who are connected directly with the Junta, feel it can be an effective and dynamic organization, and are interested in working with it. Other residents, the recent arrivals—who perhaps have not made up their minds about remaining in Tulcán, or have come to live there as only a temporary measure—usually do not wish to involve themselves. The "early" residents are the ones who continually go to Popayán as members of delegations, who are self-appointed chiefs of mingas, and who make constructive suggestions to members of the Junta's executive council. Generally, these people serve or have served as members of this governing body. The installation of street lights, improvements in water service, and enlargement and renovation of the sewer and bridge have been and will be due largely to their efforts.

TULCANESES AND THE MUNICIPAL AND
DEPARTMENTAL GOVERNMENTS

Tulcaneses say that they are a forgotten and neglected lot. They call the municipal government a "centralist" regime which is concerned only with the needs of those who live in the center of Popayán, and they resent the fact that the government's energies appear to be directed at repairing sidewalks in the center of town while the streets in the peripheral poor barrios remain unpaved. Yet, they say, while the poor are the last to receive government assistance, they are the first to be adversely affected whenever the local government decides to do such things as license small businesses or improve the "aesthetic" quality of Popayán by removing sidewalk vendors.

In August 1970, a change of national administration occurred which resulted in a new governor for Cauca and a new mayor for Popayán, and Tulcaneses hoped they would benefit from it. At first this seemed to be the case. Within his first month in office, the new mayor held a meeting of all the Junta presidents of poor barrios around Popayán, listening to their grievances and receiving petitions for municipal assistance. Shortly thereafter, city trucks began arriving in the barrio loaded with fill for the rutty streets. People talked about completing the barrio sewer and repairing the bridge leading into the barrio, and other new projects for improving the area were suggested. However, after, several months, little actually had been done, and hopes waned a bit. Tulcaneses shrugged off the delays and promises of better things to come, saying they were used to unfulfilled pledges from both local and national governments. A credibility gap has always existed for them.

Perhaps the primary reason for their relative apathy toward municipal and departmental governments lies in the selection of these officials. In Colombia, the president appoints the governor of each department and territory, who in turn names the mayors of the cities and towns under his jurisdiction. Tulcaneses have no say and, unlike power brokers in the center of town, exert no influence in filling these positions.

NATIONAL POLITICS: AN APPEAL TO THE PAST
AND THE FUTURE

In spite of their disinterest in barrio politics and their lack of influence on the municipal and departmental political structures, Tulcaneses are by no means apolitical. On the contrary, as with almost all Colombians, national politics interest them greatly, and political conversations among barrio men are noisy and volatile. The political interest of the proletariat goes back a good many years. The progressive "New Deal" administration of Alfonso López in the 1930s (Dix 1967:77–78), which included the passage of Colombia's land reform bill of 1936 (Hirschman 1963:96), brought about changes that demonstrated the power of the political process to aid heretofore disenfranchised elements of society, and the simultaneous "resurrection" of the Liberal party (Fals 1969:137) created a political base for this element. During the years from 1930 to 1948 the Liberal party became a people's party, in part due to the following of an industrial, urban middle class, and in part through efforts of New Deal Liberals to capitalize on a developing political awareness among the urban and rural poor (Hobsbawm 1963:29). The emergence of Jorge Eliécer Gaitán as a spokesman for the poor and his subsequent violent death precipitated two decades of civil strife and created a further cognizance, albeit a bloody one, of the political world. These events brought about a political awareness which, with the help of mass communications, continues today.

A primary indication of Tulcanés political involvement was the participation in the April 1970 presidential elections, in which 65 per cent of the 275 barrio household heads voted. Table 7–1 presents information about these households heads: The level of literate Tulcanés voters was higher than the barrio average, as was the percentage of male voters, whose participation proportionately exceeded that of female household heads. Payanés-born residents showed a greater tendency to vote than did migrants. Household heads who were the primary breadwinners voted in greater numbers proportionately than those who were not, as did those household heads who earned more than the barrio average. For all barrio inhabitants twenty-one and older, the voter turnout was somewhat less impressive; nevertheless, although only 53 per cent of those of voting age cast ballots (Table 7–2), this figure is higher than the national turnout of previous years. Nearly two-thirds of those who did not vote said that they would have voted and wanted to, but were unable to meet residency requirements in Popayán or were unable to furnish proper papers when they tried to vote. Certainly the percentage of registered voters who actually voted is high.

Although all mass media together may be credited for the

TABLE 7-1

Characteristics of Household Heads Who Voted
in the April 19, 1970, Elections

Characteristic	No. Who Voted	% of Total in Each Category Who Voted
Education		
Literate (N=199)	133	66.8
Illiterate (N=76)	46	60.5
Sex		
Men (N=228)	154	67.5
Women (N=47)	25	53.2
Area of origin		
Popayán (N=57)	42	73.7
Other (N=218)	137	62.8
Household head is chief breadwinner		
Yes (N=208)	139	66.8
No (N=67)	40	59.7
Travel experience		
Been to Cali (N=213)	145	68.1
Been to Bogotá (N=72)	55	76.4
Outside Colombia (N=12)	10	83.1
Household head income		
Above $350/month (N=108)	77	71.3
Below $350/month (N=167)	102	61.1
Property status		
Owners (N=182)	126	69.2
Renters (N=84)	46	54.8
Squatters (N=9)	7	77.8

high political participation of Colombians, it is primarily the transistor radio that keeps Tulcaneses abreast of national and international events. A single radio, operating continuously, may serve three or four households. In contrast, newspapers play a minor role in the dissemination of information, for the price of 1 peso makes them too expensive for most families to purchase on a daily basis, and they are not sold in Tulcán. Television is prohibitively expensive for most families; as I have noted, there is only one set in the barrio.

Perhaps the most potent force for political awareness among Tulcaneses in 1970 was the ANAPO political party, the Alianza Nacional Popular (National Popular Alliance). Its as-

TABLE 7-2

Barrio Voter Participation

	Males	Females	Total
Voted	N = 198 (63.1%)	N = 148 (43.5%)	N = 346 (52.9%)
Did not vote	N = 116 (36.9%)	N = 192 (56.5%)	N = 308 (47.1%)
Total of voting age residents	N = 314 (48.0%)	N = 340 (52.0%)	N = 654 (100.0%)

tute courtship of the poor was guided by former dictator (1953–57) and retired army general Gustavo Rojas Pinilla. A conservative, Rojas united politicians of various political and philosophical beliefs allied in their opposition to the Frente Nacional (National Front), a coalition of Liberals and Conservatives whose governments have alternately ruled Colombia since 1958. Because of the general's ill health, ANAPO in reality was led by his daughter, María Eugenia Rojas de Morales, a woman with the charismatic appeal of Eva Perón and the political shrewdness of Indira Gandhi. In the 1970 elections ANAPO largely eliminated the Liberal and Conservative basis of support among the poor classes and took on the role of their protector in the political power structure by convincing them that the government had the means and resources to alleviate their problems, and it was up to the poor to force them to do so.

Rojas' campaign and the support he received from Tulcaneses illustrate the extent of politicization of the poor. At election time, evidence of his appeal was widespread in Tulcán; posters showing the general in military dress and bearing the slogan "Social Justice and Economic Retention" appeared throughout the barrio, and a Rojas committee was formed which claimed total support of the residents. All over the barrio there was talk that Rojas was sure to win and that his victory meant better times for the poor. In Tulcán, from all appearances, Rojas was the only candidate.

During the campaign, Rojas appeared at a rally in Popayán and said that during his previous administration, money was allocated for building a road connecting Popayán to the coast. This, he noted, would have provided the poor with numerous jobs, but before construction could begin, he was removed from office "by the oligarchy." The funds were then used by the rich to build roads leading to their ranches and country estates. Then, playing upon memories of the low cost of living during his administration, Rojas held up a sack of potatoes and asked the crowd what it had cost. As they shouted and cheered, Rojas promised to sell staples for the same prices after he returned to office and, to whet their appetites still more, a truckload of food was actually sold at the old prices. His promises of full employment, a stabilized economy, and the peso at a par with the U.S. dollar were believed by almost all Tulcaneses. In short, the general pledged the rural and urban reforms which the National Front has been unsuccessful in effecting over the years.

Although Rojas' 1953–57 administration was far from a total success, even his detractors admit that some steps were taken to correct Colombia's social injustices, such as tax and land reforms, the institution of minimum wages, and public works projects to provide employment for the poor (Dix 1967:123; Szulc 1959:230). Tulcaneses, remembering the better points of his administration, and a time of relative prosperity, not surprisingly would like to turn back the calendar. Of a sample of twenty-three household heads, twenty-two indicated that they voted for Rojas; only one said he reluctantly supported the National Front's candidate, Misael Pastrana.

Since they anticipated victory, Tulcaneses were greatly upset when Rojas lost, particularly in view of the fact that, according to the preliminary count, he was beaten by less than three thousand votes out of a national total of more than three million. They felt the election was a fraud, and even some of the winner's supporters were surprised and slightly skeptical about the results. Tulcaneses assumed that the issue had not really been ended with the election. The Pastrana administration, they felt, was too inept to handle the country's problems, so it would only be a matter of time before the military stepped in and, to save the country, would award Rojas his rightful sash of office. During the turbulent spring of 1971, Tulcaneses interpreted the teachers' strike, the peasant land seizures, the nationwide work stoppage, the university student rebellion, and the escalating cost of living as sure signs that a coup d'etat was in the making. An army general who proclaimed his faith in the Pastrana government in the local newspaper only served to convince remaining skeptics. Noted Jaime Arias, "When the military starts to talk about the situation in the country, it means there is going to be a coup."

Yet, despite their dissatisfaction with the election results, Tulcaneses have not become revolutionaries: their feelings of neglect and exploitation have not led them to violence, for they realize they cannot feed and clothe their families and be revolutionaries at the same time. They are intimidated by the power structure, but at the same time, they regard some of their prospective liberators—the urban guerrillas and rebelling students who call for a "student-worker alliance"—with uncertainty and confusion. What Tulcaneses want is fulfillment of the promises Rojas made, and they look upon the aging and ailing general as their messiah. However unlikely this seems, they believe the natural forces of political evolution are on their side and if patience is what is needed—well, it is something they possess in abundance.

8. Medical and Religious Institutions

TULCÁN is built on a low-lying, swampy stretch of land between two streams, and after rains, pools of water remain for hours or even days. Dampness penetrates the houses, and for those who sleep on straw mats on dirt floors, respiratory infections seem the rule rather than the exception. Environmental sanitation, as we have seen, leaves much to be desired. More than a quarter of the homes have neither indoor toilet nor outdoor latrine, so fly-borne diseases are common. In fact, in the space of five months—January–May 1971—nine children, all under the age of four, died from bronchially related infections.

Poverty contributes to the lack of environmental sanitation in Tulcán and causes the other conditions that give rise to poor health: inadequate diet, insufficient clothing, and lack of money to consult doctors and purchase medicines. In addition, the persistence of folk medical beliefs sometimes aggravates the seriousness of illness, for although Tulcaneses know that physicians can at times work wondrous cures, they also believe that *mal de ojo*, or *ojo bravo* (evil eye), *susto* (fright), *tristeza* (sadness), and witchcraft are best treated by folk medical curers. Consequently, patients diagnosed as suffering from such ailments are taken to physicians only as a last resort, often when it is too late for medical help. Finally, there is general ignorance of the rules of hygiene. Although people talk about germs and parasites and know that they cause illness, still there is an overall lack of understanding about what they are, how they transmit disease, and what can be done to control them. Dishwashing is perfunctory at best, the protection of food from flies is of secondary interest, and the disposal of organic waste is carelessly done.

Because of poverty, most people's diets consist mainly of inexpensive, starchy foods such as plantains, yuca, and potatoes, with insufficient amounts of animal protein and the vitamins that are found in fresh fruits and vegetables. Hernán Granada feeds his family of eight on his meager earnings of 5 or 6 pesos a day. Like many other poor families, they eat only twice a day: bread and coffee in the morning and, in midafternoon, a stew of yuca and plantains flavored with bits of the cheapest meats. Not surprisingly, the Granada children have spindly legs and bloated stomachs and are often sick. While the Granadas are among the poorest barrio families, there are a great many others that are little better nourished.

Insufficient income for clothing also affects the health. Hookworms spread because children do not wear shoes, and tetanus is a constant threat for the same reason. Few families have sufficient clothing to be able to make a complete change when they come in from the rain; consequently, they shiver until body heat dries them. Many people have inadequate clothing for keeping warm on cold nights, and colds and pneumonia are common.

Finally, when people are sick they cannot afford to stop working because they have so few monetary reserves. Therefore, since they cannot rest and perhaps throw off an infection in its early stages, all too often an illness runs a full and lengthy course.

MEDICAL TREATMENT

When Tulcaneses seek medical help, they have several options. One is the barrio health center, a one-room building located on the edge of the school grounds. It is run by a French-Canadian nurse, Jacques Le Carré, who purchases medicines with contributions made by friends and relatives in Canada. Le Carré, who has operated the health center since 1969, does not charge for his services and medicines, but those patients who can are expected to leave a peso or two. Every afternoon between two and five o'clock, the center's formal hours, patients come for the simple help Le Carré can offer. And on Saturday afternoons, a Popayán physician spends two hours attending the more difficult cases screened for him by the nurse.

People also go to other clinics and doctors, and to the city hospital for treatment. Nearby Barrio Alfonso López has a free government clinic, as does Barrio Chuni, and Tulcaneses sometimes go to one of these when Le Carré is not in Tulcán. Patent medicines and antibiotics are available without prescription in drugstores, and although mistakes undoubtedly occur, individuals become very adept at choosing medicines for themselves and their families. Furthermore, they may consult pharmacists in Popayán, who occupy a role much closer to that of a medical doctor in diagnosing and prescribing medicines than do their North American counterparts. Tulcaneses place a great deal of faith in these individuals.

Practically any adult in the barrio can give injections, and many families have their own hypodermic syringes which they readily lend to neighbors. For a number of years, Micaela de Miranda has been one of the foremost experts in "applying injections." She diagnoses the illness and tells the individual what type of medicine he should procure in the pharmacy. This is brought to her and, for a nominal fee, she administers the injection. As a rule, injections are regarded as very powerful, and when the choice is between an injection or a pill, the needle always is preferred. If the remedy is good, a little pain should accompany the cure, it is reasoned.

There are also people in the barrio who, while not formally considered to be curers, nonetheless are recognized as specialists in home remedies. They will prescribe a herb tea for stomach cramps or "pains in the liver," more than likely gathering the necessary ingredients in their own gardens. There are also folk medical curers in the barrio, like Samuel Méndez, who calls himself a *yerbatero* (herbalist) and *curandero* (curer) and specializes in botanical remedies. He is often consulted for infirmities ranging from sore throats and rheumatism to the evil eye and witchcraft. He also doubles as the local orthopedic specialist, setting broken bones and tending dislocated joints.

Having originally learned his trade from his mother, a curandera in Popayán, Samuel is a dedicated student of medicine. He reads anything on curing he can obtain and proudly shows his prized possessions—two Red Cross books on first aid which a friend salvaged from the trash behind the public health building in Popayán. On particularly difficult cases, Samuel may consult other practitioners who live in the area, sometimes recommending a patient to another curer, and in return often getting referral clients from his colleagues. Although curers like Samuel generally deal in and recommend botanical remedies, they are also familiar with numerous patent medicines and do not hesitate to prescribe them alone or in conjunction with a herbal remedy.

Tulcaneses also consult spiritists who reside in the area. As its name implies, spiritism is curing through the use of spirits (cf. Kelly 1961), and Tulcaneses have access to practitioners of two types of spiritism. "Celestial spiritism" takes place while the patient lies on the floor in a hypnotic trance. The spiritist, called brother, implores the Virgin and the saints to perform the operation necessary to cure the individual of his illness, pain, or discomfort. Afterwards, the patient is awakened and told to go home; he can expect to arise cured on the following day.

The second type, "spiritism of the light," is practiced by a barrio resident, Marco Astaiza. Dressed in pure white "to facilitate communications," he goes into what he calls a "cataleptic trance"—accomplished by consuming large quantities of aguardiente—and calls upon the spirits of the dead to inform him of the nature of the patient's illness and what he must take to be cured. A medium (in Marco's case, his Francisca) writes down the name of the malady and the prescribed remedy as the spiritist relays it from the spirit. In some instances, a diabolic spirit may try to intervene, and the helper must protect the defenseless spiritist by hitting him on the ribs and forearms, thus driving away the evil spirit. Spiritists of both types practice only on Tuesdays and Fridays, days considered auspicious.

Two midwives live in the barrio. However, because of the

proximity of the city hospital and its charity maternity ward, women favor leaving the barrio for their deliveries, and the midwives are summoned only in times of emergency. However, during pregnancy, many women visit the midwives for advice and massages. When she was pregnant with her third child, Elodia Arroyo was told by a midwife that she was going to have a difficult delivery. When the time came, Elodia checked into the hospital, where doctors performed a Caesarean section. Perhaps Marta de Cruz best characterized the feelings of barrio women when she said, "Frankly, the hospital is the only place where you should give birth. There they have doctors who can take care of any problems which might occur."

Sibundoy Indians from southern Colombia are also consulted, either in Popayán's main market or when they make their periodic rounds through the barrio itself. Tulcaneses purchase protective amulets and herbs directly from them, and they also supply curers with otherwise hard-to-find herbs, bear paws, tapir hooves, toucan peaks, snakeskins, and other essential and esoteric paraphernalia used in curing. In a sense, the Sibundoys are to the curer what the pharmaceutical company is to the drugstore.

Unlike what Press (1969, 1971) has described for Bogotá, none of the barrio practitioners has anything resembling an office where he (or she) sees patients or maintains office hours. In general, practitioners are available for consultation at any time, although individuals who seek treatment from the barrio spiritist must come to Marco's house at eight in the evening, as that is the time when he is best able to communicate with the spirits.

In addition to consulting with practitioners in the barrio, Tulcaneses may visit at least six different *centros de espiritismo* (spiritist centers) or *misiones santisimas* (holy missions) located in town, usually in low-income areas of the city. Here spiritists addressed as *"Hermano"* (brother) or *"Hermana"* (sister) beseech the saints to cure the sick and infirm. Hermano José's center in Barrio Alfonso López is one such clinic. On Tuesdays and Fridays, beginning shortly before three in the afternoon, people enter his house—unmarked, inconspicuous, and indistinguishable on the outside from those surrounding it. Hermano José's patio, covered by two plexiglass skylights, serves as a chapel for the curing ceremonies. Wooden benches and chairs, enough to accommodate forty to fifty people, occupy approximately three-quarters of the patio with an altar taking up the remaining space. The walls in the nave, where the people are seated, contain numerous religious pictures; interpersed among them are written testimonies from people who have been cured by Hermano José. Many are written on *papel sellado* (a special form on which all legal negotiations are spelled out), as if to rule out any possibility of someone claiming anything less than the complete truth.

The altar is crowded with various-sized pictures of the Virgin Mary, Jesus Christ, and various saints, especially with reproductions of Fray David, San Roque, and San Gregorio —those relied on most often by Hermano José. Vases of flowers—some fresh, others plastic—occupy little niches in the altar, and strings of blinking lights surround an almost life-size picture of the Virgin.

From three until three-thirty Hermano José, dressed in a white smock and grey flannel slacks, prays in the chancel, calling upon the spirits to "enter" him and aid him in curing the assembled. At approximately three-thirty the "cleansing" begins. In groups of seven, people are invited into the sanctuary and arranged in a semicircle. Hermano José, now thoroughly possessed by the saints, whispers a prayer and then says, "Sickness, leave; health, enter" as he anoints each with some "baptized" and perfumed water. When he finishes, he returns to the first one and, breathing heavily, his body quivering, closes his eyes and runs his hands down the sides of each patient three or four times. Each pass terminates with a quick flip of the wrist resulting in a loud cracking sound as his fingers snap together. When he does this the members of the congregation audibly suck in their breath, almost as if they can see him strip illness out of the patients and shake it off his fingers. With a wooden cross he next blesses each person, once on the front and then on the back. When he is finished, an assistant comes forward and gives each participant a shotglass of "purified" water. Cleansed, they leave, perhaps stopping on their way out to fill a bottle they brought with holy water and dropping something in the collection box. As they leave, another group takes their place in the altar area. This continues for several hours until everyone has been treated.

Hermano José has a *consultorio* (examining room) off the patio where he treats patients. A large desk, stacked with piles of papers, takes up one corner. The shelves and filing cabinets which line the walls are cluttered with jars and vials containing various liquid and solid remedies. Books, magazines, and patients' files are jammed and wedged into any available space. The walls are covered with religious pictures and human anatomy charts.

Here Hermano José consults with his patients. While he draws blood, checks blood pressure and pulse, examines urine samples, and interviews patients about their ailments, his wife, Hermana Patricia, collects medical histories. Remedies, both botanical and pharmaceutical, may be prescribed and the patient is charged according to several criteria—among them ability to pay, number of visits necessary to insure a cure, and types of remedies used.

CONSIDERATIONS IN THE CHOICE OF MEDICINES AND CONSULTATION

How do people decide what sort of medicines to take and what types of consultation to seek? Answers to these questions are based on a combination of convenience, accessibility, financial situation,[1] and past experience—and of course, depending upon the illness, specific types of advice and cures are recognized as superior to others.

Tulcaneses feel that physicians are unable to recognize most folk illnesses and, as one Tulcanés suggested, medical doctors are quite liable "to diagnose someone suffering from susto as being an epileptic." It is not unusual for Tulcaneses to seek treatment from physicians, then shift to folk practitioners, and vice versa. Some even consult both sources simultaneously. Jorge Cruz visited social security physicians a number of times for recurring headaches and dizziness. Unable to get relief, he eventually sought treatment from a curandero highly

1. With few exceptions, the cost of medicine from barrio medical personnel is a fraction of what physicians in Popayán charge: 50 to 200 pesos per visit, depending on the doctor and whether it is an office or home call. Curanderos charge by the ailment, frequently depending on the success of the cure. This may range from a couple of pesos to a high of 70 pesos. Spiritists are more expensive, their fees being comparable to those of physicians.

recommended by Miguel Ordóñez, who at the time was being treated for a case of witchcraft. In other instances, Darío Ramos and Carmen de Aguirre both went to spiritists for treatment, he for a back ailment which a medical doctor was going to charge him a large sum of money to treat and she for a cure for her daughter's susto after realizing that physicians would not be able to cure it.

In many respects, a rather harmonious relationship exists between patent and home medicines. Often they are used together, as when a curandero recommends a tea five times a day made from *verdolaga blanca* (white purslane) to be taken with "Aspirina Bayer." In spite of this relationship, it is widely believed that for certain illnesses only herbs can be used with success, and for treating others it would be foolish to use anything but patent medicines. Hernán Granada feels that scientific technology has produced many new illnesses, none of which is curable with plant remedies. This feeling is shared by many who are convinced that such phenomena as nuclear testing and exploration of space cause new types of maladies through parthenogenesis. Still, as if to even the score, Tulcaneses are also convinced that there are illnesses on which patent medicines have no effect.

Common infirmities, such as stomachaches and colds, are treated with home remedies. These ailments have agreed-upon hot and cold characteristics, and residents deal with them accordingly (cf. Currier 1966; Ingham 1970). For example, stomach pains are believed to result from excess cold, and treatment consists of teas made from plants with hot or warm qualities, while fevers, believed to be caused by an overabundance of heat, are treated with plant brews which have cold or fresh properties. Colds, as the name implies in both English and Spanish, come from too much cold, and naturally the antidotes are warm ones. Nevertheless, in spite of the agreement on the intrinsic qualities of the abovementioned maladies, there is a general lack of agreement on the hot-cold qualities of most others. When queried, some of the most erudite people in botanical curing simply state that they do not know the qualities of most of the illnesses they treat and, furthermore, do not feel that this is a very important factor in diagnosis and treatment.

FOLK ILLNESSES

An understanding of folk illnesses, or at least an awareness of their existence, their causes, and how they are treated, sheds more light on the world view and ethos of Tulcaneses than practically any other topic.

The evil eye (mal de ojo, or ojo bravo), one of the illnesses believed to be immune to patent medicines, heads the list. Tulcaneses feel that evil eye is caused by envy, and although theoretically both men and women can posses it, the only people actually believed to have it are women. Evil eye is an innate quality with which some people are born, many of whom are never aware they possess it. It should not be confused with witchcraft, for the latter is learned and, in most cases, employed intentionally and in a mischievous and harmful manner. Only small children and animals are susceptible to the evil eye, and after the age of six or seven, a child is felt to be large enough to defend himself so that he is no longer in danger.

There are two types of evil eye: the standard eye and the fool's eye. The standard variety is a fast-acting illness, and after being "eyed," the child usually dies within three to five hours, following vomiting and diarrhea. There are two methods for treating this type of evil eye. The person thought responsible puts her saliva in the child's mouth and on its navel. This causes the child to fall into a deep sleep and awake fully recovered. If the act is unintentional, as is usually the case, cooperation from the "eyer" presents no problem. If the "eyer" is unknown, the child is given three teaspoons of heated *cimarrón* (bitter *mate*) juice into which a *cabalonga negra* (black bean) seed has been dropped, stirred three times, and promptly removed. Because the seed is reputed to be poisonous, the solution is thought to kill the child if it remains too long. The juice produces a deep sleep and, upon awakening, the child is cured.

Fool's eye is so named because the ill child moves like a drunkard or a fool. Afflicted by this type of evil eye, a child may linger for weeks or months before finally dying from what "appears" to be malnutrition. But a person who knows what to look for can tell if the victim has fool's eye because one of its eyes will be more closed than the other. If detected in its early stages, the cimarrón juice remedy may be used, or a woman pregnant with her *first* child can produce a cure by putting her saliva in the child's mouth and navel once a day for nine straight days. People are not sure why it must be a woman expecting her first baby, but they know from experience that other women do not have this curative power.

Children are protected against the evil eye by amulets hung around their wrists. These bracelets, sold by Sibundoy Indians, generally consist of a black thread on which dangles an *azabache*, a black "seed" carved in the shape of a clenched fist, often with the thumb protruding between the index and middle fingers. For additional good luck, the bracelet may include an enamel medallion of the Virgin, although this is believed to be of questionable value as an amulet. An azabache protects a child by diverting the force of the "eye" from the child's gall to the azabache, which breaks in two and, in so doing, saves the child's life. Thus, parents who discover an offspring with a broken azabache realize just how close the child has been to death.

Tulcaneses say the quality of the azabache can be tested by pulling a hair from the head, sticking the root to the azabache, and lighting it with a match: if the hair burns, the azabache is worthless. After Cecilia de Burgos' three-year-old daughter, Elsa, died from what Cecilia is sure was the evil eye, she lamented that she had failed to test her daughter's azabache. Cecilia is convinced that a good azabache would have saved the girl's life.

A second and less frequently used amulet is an old piece of silver money, which the child wears on a string around its neck. The money can be of any denomination, notes one resident, "as long as it is at least ten years old, because as everyone knows, since that time the government has not minted any 'real' money."

When individuals know they have the evil eye—or are afraid they may be accused of having it—they keep it from "penetrating," i.e., damaging, by slapping any child upon which they may gaze on the buttocks and saying, "May God watch over you; nothing will happen." In this way, potential malice is believed abated, since anyone envious of a child would not hurt it. Commending the child into God's care is another safety precaution.

Animals as well as children are susceptible to the evil eye, but since Tulcaneses know of no amulets to protect them, the best policy for a visitor is simply not to admire his host's animals. Faustina de Arias once had a pair of songbirds of which she was very proud. One afternoon, a neighbor remarked on how beautifully they sang, and within a short time both were dead—obvious victims, Faustina says, of the evil eye.

Witchcraft also plays a part in the Tulcanés sociomedical world view. Although not all witchcraft is bad—with it, women may enforce the faithfulness of absent husbands—usually it is of an evil and malicious variety. Tulcaneses recognize two types of evil witchcraft: *trastorno*, or magical fright, and *carate*, which produces open sores that spread over the victim's body. Envious people cause both of these illnesses when, under the guise of friendship, they prescribe special herbs containing bewitching potions for colds or provide ointments containing a hexing agent for burns or cuts. It requires some knowledge of witchcraft to cure victims of bewitchings.

Susto (fright) and *espanto* (i.e., fright which implies soul loss) are also believed to be immune to patent medicines and, as with evil eye, unrecognizable by medical doctors. A variety of frightening experiences may cause susto, such as a bee sting, a bad dream, an encounter with a snake, or having a close call with any grave danger. In order to cure susto, a curandero must first discover what caused the fright. Usually he then uses a folk remedy such as a tea made from *cedrón* (sage), *toronjil* (balm gentle), or *limoncillo* (small lemon), to treat the symptoms and bring the individual out of the sluggish, lethargic stupor produced by susto. Samuel Méndez concocts a more complicated antidote by mixing eleven different herbs and plants, and the shavings from a tapir's hoof and from a toucan's beak, in half a liter of aguardiente.

Tristeza or *causato* (sadness) is caused by the death or disappearance of a loved one; it occurs most often among children, although it also afflicts adults. Patients suffering from tristeza do not eat, their hair falls out, and they constantly chew on their fingernails. To cure tristeza, a little foresight is needed. A lock of hair is taken from the deceased and saved for such a contingency, and when a member of the family shows signs of tristeza, the hair is burned, put into a drink, and given to the ailing one. In addition, the family must move from the place where the death occurred.

Elodia Arroyo's six-year-old daughter died of tristeza three months after her one-year-old sister died. Although Elodia gave the girl a potion with the burned hair in it, they did not change residences; therefore, the cure was not completed. When the doctor signed the death certificate, he listed the cause of death as malnutrition, but, notes Elodia, that was because the child would not eat due to the tristeza.

Witchcraft, susto, tristeza, and the evil eye provide Tulcaneses with sociopsychologically acceptable explanations for deaths which perhaps are due more to economic impoverishment than to anything else. They also provide a means for explaining envy and serve as a buffer against social transgressions. Folk illnesses simply serve to explain to Tulcaneses the otherwise unexplainable.

RELIGIOUS INSTITUTIONS

For Tulcaneses, the interrelationship of medical and religious institutions is obvious, for spirits, the intervention of saints, faith in the protection of a benevolent Almighty, and prayers provide common denominators for both subjects. Life in Tulcán has a capricious quality, and many things happen over which the people have no direct control. These include the proper amounts of rain and sun for crops, clients coming to hire carts for the day, luck in getting a job on a construction site, the recovery of a sick member of the family, the fidelity of a spouse, or perhaps drawing a lucky number in the lottery of Quindío. The faithful can try to control such events, at least in part, by calling on the supernatural.

THE CHURCH AND THE BARRIO

Every Sunday morning, mass is said in the barrio's community center by one of the French-Canadian priests who live and work in the Barrio Alfonso López. Attendance has never been high, but because people may attend services at various hours and at different churches in town, no one is sure how many Tulcaneses attend mass regularly. In the barrio, there are no social pressures to go, and many admit they do not.

Not long ago, in an effort to draw more people to church,

three changes were made. First, the bishop replaced one of the Canadian priests who was relatively new to Popayán and not yet fluent in Spanish with another who had lived and worked in the area for over a year, speaks good Spanish, and personally knows many of Tulcán's residents. Second, the hour of mass was changed from nine to ten o'clock in the hope that the later hour would make it more convenient for late-night celebrants. And finally, the location of the service was switched from the barrio school to the community center, which is more centrally located and equipped with more comfortable seats. These changes appear to have met with some success, for local attendance has risen.

One current barrio project is to build a chapel next to the school and the health center, and for the past year, a committee has been working to raise money, draw up plans, and promote general barrio interest and support. In spite of this praiseworthy goal, Andrea de Arenas feels, with good reason, that it will be years before anything is done: she has been on the committee for the past year, and they have held only one meeting in all that time.

Although Tulcán is part of the Alfonso López parish, people prefer to have their children baptized and confirmed in Santo Domingo or San Francisco, churches in Popayán, even though they must give false addresses to do so. Tulcaneses consider Alfonso López to be a low-class barrio, and they prefer the elaborate and more prestigious churches in the center of town to the rather simple, drab Alfonso López chapel.

In order to encourage an interest in religion and a feeling of community, nuns from the Popayán school San José de Tarbas have been holding a barrio Christmas *novena* for the past two years. Each afternoon from December 16 to 24, a group of women and children, along with a couple of nuns and some young girls from San José, gather in front of a house in the barrio, and for half an hour, they sing Christmas carols and "pray to the baby Jesus." The nuns select a different house for each day and loan plaster-of-paris nativity figures of Mary, Joseph, Jesus, and farm animals so that the members of the household may construct a nativity scene with moss and flowers from the surrounding hills. Thus, a religious "tradition" has been started in the barrio.

ACCIÓN CATÓLICA

Acción Católica, a socioreligious lay organization sponsored by upper-class Payanés women, has a number of female participants from the barrio. Once a week, women from Popayán meet with women from Tulcán to talk about their problems, to socialize, and to squeeze in a little religious training, emphasizing mainly the desirability of marriage for Tulcanés women living in free unions. For the women from Tulcán, these meetings not only provide pleasant breaks in their daily routine, but also have some fringe benefits. At various intervals, if their attendance is deemed satisfactory, the women receive used clothes, food, and other household items, and if a woman has a baby while she is a member of Acción Católica, she receives a basket containing six diapers, six small blankets, a sweater, two pairs of knit shoes, a small jacket, antidiaper-rash medicine, a bar of soap for babies, and a thick blanket —quite a windfall for a poor family.

Being part of this organization provides lower-class women with potentially powerful patrons (generally unavailable to them) since Tulcaneses come into contact with upper-class women in an informal manner through their participation. These women help their lower-class associates if their requests are not too great and are made in connection with the organization. Assistance from upper-class women in Acción Católica made it possible for Angelina de Ordóñez to send her twenty-four-year-old son, who was suffering from magical fright, to a mental hospital in Pasto; similarly, Micaela de Miranda was able to resolve a problem about her husband's working papers. In spite of these obvious advantages, women are reluctant to use this opportunity when they need it because they feel it would be bothersome and presumptuous to do so.

RELIGIOUS ACTIVITIES IN POPAYÁN

With respect to most socioreligious activities in Popayán, Tulcaneses tend to be mere spectators; when on occasion they do participate, it is as individuals and not as residents of Tulcán. Individuals in the barrio sometimes join with acquaintances from other parts of town to form *chirimía* musical bands which wander through the streets of town during the Christmas season playing traditional Payanés drum and flute music (cf. A. Whiteford 1956:8–9, 1960:114–15), but there has never been a band composed entirely of Tulcaneses. No Tulcaneses are members of the Easter *cofradías* (religious brotherhoods) which care for and prepare the *pasos* (floats) with scenes depicting the events surrounding the crucifixion, nor do they carry them in the Holy Week processions (cf. A. Whiteford 1954a, 1954b). However, on the first of May, they may become participants when they struggle for positions to carry the "worker's" paso of El Santo Ecce-Homo ("El Amo" [Christ crowned with thorns]) for a few feet.

HAGIOLATRY AND THE FEAR OF GHOSTS

Personal, informal religious activities constitute another important aspect of Tulcanés religious life. These often take place in the individual's home and concern him not as a member of any group, but as a person dealing with his own or his family's sociopsychological and religious needs. Thus, Tulcaneses seek the assistance of God, Jesus Christ, various saints, the Virgin Mary, both good and evil spirits, angels, and the devil. They may also call upon various manifestations (represented by different images) of the Virgin and the saints, all of whom provide general protection as well as having specific powers.

Some families and individuals have patron saints or a special protective Virgin on whom they rely more than others and whose responsibility they feel it is to watch over and protect them. They feel that these patrons can be relied on as long as they are remembered by regular offerings of lighted candles on church altars, through fulfillment of promises made during times of need, and perhaps by an occasional novena said in their behalf. In many households religious pictures are venerated even though the family may not be sure of the specific powers of the saint so honored. This may be thought of as a general, all-purpose insurance covering the family against practically any calamity.

To establish and maintain communications with the supernatural, many families have household altars. These range in elaborateness from a wall covered with numerous holy pictures, with lighted candles and flowers in front of them, to a single picture of Christ, a saint, or a specific Virgin seemingly lost on a dark wall, surrounded by pictures of soccer players or practically hidden from view by large, ornate calendars of past years.

Even though a family may feel that it is protected by its particular patrons, for specific problems it usually selects a Virgin or saint known to have powers that fit the particular situation. Among the favorites are La Virgen de las Lajas, La Virgen de la Playa, La Virgen del Carmen, and Nuestro Señor de Buga, a replica of Spain's famous "El Cachorro," all of whom protect and cure the sick, while San Martín de Porres is the custodian of the poor. A woman lights a candle before a picture of San Marcos when her husband is angry, in order that his rage may subside. La Mano Poderosa is called upon to calm angry neighbors, and Omnipotencia de Dios and San Martín are appealed to when individuals need work.

When evoking a saint or the Virgin through prayer, the individual may make a promise to be fulfilled if his request is granted. Often this vow is a promise to journey to a shrine or to light candles on the protector's behalf. Tulcaneses regard these requests to the supernatural not merely as exercises in charity on the part of the supernatural, but as two-way contracts. In return for an act by one party, a reciprocal deed is performed by the other. Generally speaking, this contract hinges on the supernatural doing its share first.

When Carlos Arias was twenty days old, he suddenly developed stomach problems. According to his mother, "He was alive one moment and dead the next, and he was not baptized." Fearing Carlito's soul would drift for eternity because he had not been baptized, Faustina wrapped him in a sheet and hurried to the Chapel of Bethlehem, where she placed the baby at the base of the paso of El Amo, the patron of Popayán, and asked the figure to restore the child's life. The request was granted, Carlos quickly was baptized, and now, at the age of seven, he is in fine health. Out of gratitude, Faustina daily lights a candle before a picture of El Amo, seeking his blessings and protection for her family.

It is common for Tulcaneses to make pilgrimages to the shrine of La Virgen de las Lajas in southern Colombia. Judith de Aguila has made two trips, a twenty-hour bus ride, in repayment for the Virgin's aid in times of need. Héctor Arias visited Las Lajas once while suffering from an ear infection and subsequent deafness, which curanderos and physicians alike said was incurable. Héctor entered the chapel at Las Lajas, confessed, and prayed, promising that if he were cured he would send a donation of 50 pesos and return once for the Virgin's day. The following morning when he awoke, he noticed there was no longer any pain, and by that afternoon, his hearing had been restored—clear evidence of the Virgin's powers. When he returned to Popayán, he mailed the 50 pesos, although as yet he has not fulfilled the second part of his promise.

The Virgin is said to be uncompromising in her demands for respect and fulfillment of promises made. Some years ago, a small procession was scheduled to take place in Popayán in honor of the Virgen de Fátima, and people were asked to tidy up the fronts of their houses along the route where the procession was going to pass. Elbi Muñoz let it be known he did not have time for such things and intentionally neglected the facade of his house. As the procession passed, he suddenly lost his ability to speak and for the past fifteen years has been mute, an obvious indication to all that the Virgin was displeased with his lack of respect.

There is widespread belief in apparitions among Tulcaneses; every adult knows someone who personally has encountered a spirit or ghost. For example, Madre Monte comes in the form of a beautiful woman who lures hunters and farmers into the woods to make love to her, where she kills them by sucking their blood. Once Pedro Aguila met her and barely escaped with his life. The experience was so upsetting that he was speechless for two months. Stories about *duendes* (dwarves or goblins), who carry small children off into the hills where they never again see their parents, are told to children to frighten them into behaving. Thus, Pedrito Muñoz stops crying whenever his sister Elena tells him he will be taken away by La Llorona, the spirit of a crying woman who endlessly searches for her lost child and takes other children as replacements.

Although most stories about spirits, ghosts, and the devil involve the potential loss of something or someone, there are also tales about people who gain fame and fortune through contracts with them, a popular means of explaining how people become rich. Adolfo Samboni knows a man living in Popayán who is rumored to have made a considerable fortune by entering into a pact with the devil.

The protection of supernatural powers is regarded as one of the few ways in which an individual can attempt to defend himself and his family and thus provides Tulcaneses with some means of dealing with life's unpredictable events.

9. Prospects for the Future

TULCANESES, as we have seen, regard existence as a series of difficult hurdles; they must constantly "fight" with life to conquer its many insecurities. They deal with these obstacles as best they can and rely on their ability to defend themselves, primarily by living as independently as possible and by constantly working to get ahead. These are the dominant themes which govern their actions and dictate their world view.

The idea of independence, a theme touched on throughout this study, plays a large role in the Tulcanés ethos. It is apparent in the living situation, where they discourage family ties which might compromise them financially, and in the deemphasis of compadrazgo. Everyday social networks are kept on a short-term, temporary level, yet are reciprocated carefully so that the relationship can be renewed when either party desires. They also avoid close personal friendships with their neighbors and seem unable to cooperate in a meaningful way in any large-scale barrio projects. The importance of the ideal of independence is further evidenced in speech: Tulcaneses invariably use the formal term of address, usted, in-

116

stead of the more familiar tu, even with children. Perhaps by remaining formal, they are expressing their desire not to compromise their wish to remain independent.

Importantly, Tulcaneses do not see their situation as static and unchanging. Most, by virtue of having moved in from the countryside, have demonstrated a desire not to sit idly and let life pass them by. Most residents, in fact, are quite optimistic that, given time and the coalescing of the proper circumstances, their way of life will improve—if not in their lifetime, then certainly in their children's. Interestingly, many Tulcaneses project a more buoyant attitude about their future and that of Colombia than do many of the more wealthy Payaneses, who look upon many of the actual and projected rural and urban reforms as threatening their security.

Tulcaneses see several ways for getting ahead. Education is the most important of these; for many it is the key with which they hope to break out of their engulfing poverty. Even though it does not seem to work wonders, as previously mentioned, they are confident that it is one of the best possible solutions and continually emphasize its importance to their children. Also, in 1970–71 they looked at Colombia's political course as being geared toward creating a better life for the poor. This was particularly true regarding the aging ex-general, ex-president Rojas. Yet, even without him, many are confident that the natural course of political evolution is on their side. Although not as important as the first two processes, luck is looked upon as another possibility for bettering themselves. Tomorrow, they reason, their fortunes may change for the better, perhaps when they win a lottery or finally get a steady job.

EMPLOYMENT IN THE FUTURE

Aside from their own ability to influence their situations, in 1970–71 changes were being planned for Popayán which could positively affect Tulcaneses' lives. Some of these will concern employment prospects.

In an attempt to alleviate the problems of unemployment, several Colombian governmental agencies are working together to establish an artisan community just outside Popayán. Its purpose will be to provide an apprentice program in pottery making, wood carving, leather working, weaving, and jewelry making, as well as to furnish a cooperative for the distribution of finished products to national and international markets (cf. Rico Castillo and Rey 1969). Should these plans be realized, many new openings will be available to Tulcán's jobless.

Industrial expansion in Popayán may improve the employment picture for the poor as well. Carvajal y Compañia, a Cali-based manufacturer of paper supplies, has purchased an old seminary and is expected to begin production in Popayán in the near future. According to reports in the local newspaper, Carvajal will invest 2 million pesos in Popayán over the next five years, and the plant eventually will employ 500 people, 98 per cent of whom will be women. Undoubtedly more industry will be attracted to Popayán because of its pleasant climate and location, since opposition among the city's power brokers to industrial development in the Pubenza Valley is diminishing. Due to a changing social climate and the efforts of the government land reform program, Instituto Colombiano de la Reforma Agraria (INCORA), wealthy families will no longer be able to retain their large landholdings; they must take the initiative in the establishment of local industry if they wish to have any voice in the city's future. Therefore, the prospects that Popayán will not remain a nonindustrialized city are increasingly good.

A CHANGING BARRIO

Change is taking place in Tulcán as well. Since its first weeks, barrio residents have deluged the city council with requests ranging from a cafeteria for the school to permanent street lights. The municipality has responded to these appeals with promises of action, but in fact, until August 1970, its officers were seriously considering razing the barrio and building an entirely new residential area in its place. These plans were abandoned for reasons of financial and political expediency: the city council apparently realized that there would be an insurrection if it tried to implement such an undertaking, and money was short anyway. Instead, the city has agreed to improve general living conditions, and both the municipal government and ICT have ambitious plans for the barrio.

The city's plans for Tulcán include improvement of the streets so that they eventually may be surfaced with cement,

FIGURE 6. Resident with vegetable stand located at barrio's entrance.

widening and strengthening the bridge at the barrio's entrance, and improving the aqueduct system so that residents will have water at all times during the day. There are also plans for a sewer system with storm drains, and since the sewage will empty into the barrio's two streams, work will be done to eliminate the problem of periodic flooding.

If the city's projected improvements seem ambitious, so are those of ICT, which plans to build eighty houses in previously unoccupied areas of the barrio. These dwellings will go to squatters and renters in Tulcán. Another aspect of the ICT design is to divide the barrio's largest blocks with roads, and line them with more new houses. Finally, ICT would like to effect block-by-block renovation to improve the barrio's existing dwellings by providing long-term, low-interest loans to homeowners, who otherwise would be unable to finance such improvements.

With few exceptions, residents are receptive to both ICT and city plans and look forward to being able to make improvements they are unable to finance at present. The local newspaper has carried various articles on the projects, the radio stations have periodic announcements about them, and residents are confident that these plans are not just like the unfulfilled promises they have heard in the past.

At the same time, many Tulcaneses are worried about how ICT's plans will affect them. The barrio's agriculturalists fear losing their main source of livelihood if their lots are reduced too much. The projected monthly house payments of 30 pesos ($1.50 U.S.) are a great deal of money to the poorest, and many are concerned about falling behind and being evicted. Although ICT has repeatedly assured them this will not be the case, it is rumored that residents in ICT housing elsewhere in Popayán have lost their homes for this reason.

On another level, change is continuously occurring in Tulcán. Houses are being built privately on empty lots at the rate of two or three a month. When individuals move out of the barrio, they almost always leave behind property which has appreciated in value because of improvements they have made. Thus, there is an accompanying trend toward slightly more affluent people moving into the barrio. Changes are taking place even without government help, and over the next few years this trend of improving the quality of houses un-doubtedly will continue. If the government does implement its plans, this will hasten the changes. In any case, within a few years some other area will probably usurp Tulcán's position as Popayán's poorest barrio.

10. Continuity and Change: 1971–74

M Y FRIEND," I was assured, "when you come back here you won't recognize this place." So confident was the speaker that the municipal and departmental governments would comply with a series of planned improvements for the barrio, he wagered a liter of aguardiente. I accepted, actually hoping it would be my bottle we would consume when we next met. Ignacio was speaking not only for himself, but for the thoughts, desires, and needs of most of Tulcán's residents.

THE BARRIO IN 1974

In June 1974, eager to see how the barrio had progressed, I returned to do a follow-up study of Tulcán. Although in fact a number of changes have occurred, at first glance it looked as it had three years earlier. There were, however, some physical modifications. The bridge leading into the barrio has been rebuilt and another small one added, thus allowing Tulcán to be included in the municipal bus network. In large measure this service has alleviated many of the nagging transportation difficulties.

The leaning bamboo electrical poles have been replaced

with concrete ones. The presence of a new transformer on the edge of the barrio now provides residents with a continuous source of power.

Other physical changes are evident. Every day trucks and horse-drawn carts move the worldly possessions of people into and out of the barrio. More than once, in talks with residents, someone would comment on the movement of people and how they knew so few of their neighbors. While the net gain of inhabitants was probably no more than 100 individuals, the constant turnover of perhaps as much as a third of the population[1] created a situation of interpersonal relations similar to what might occur if the barrio were rapidly increasing in size.

A proliferation of cantinas has greatly changed the character of Tulcán's main street. In 1970–71 there were four or five houses which on weekends played loud music and dispensed alcoholic beverages. By 1974 this number probably had tripled. At least two have jukeboxes, and on Saturday afternoons, Sundays, and sometimes Mondays they provide space for customers to dance and drink. The entire ambience of Calle 17 has also changed. In 1970–71 weekends were relatively quiet, with the cantinas providing the only real exceptions. Not only has the number of sources of noise and imbibing increased, but the number of drunks roaming the barrio's streets has multiplied. Thus, Tulcán's previous serene image is now a forgotten one.

Although the barrio has undergone such outward changes, these did not include all of those scheduled. The one which would have had the most impact never fully materialized. In 1973, after completing its initial study of the housing situation, drawing up plans for the barrio, and getting approval from Bogotá, ICT abandoned its project. The reason was quite simple. In order for work to begin, the Institute needed access to land titles, and from the beginning the agency encountered difficulties in this endeavor. Due to the chain of legal, semilegal and extralegal documentation, complicated and individualized negotiations would have had to be conducted with each owner. ICT concluded that this made the project prohibitively expensive, and the scheme was never realized. For residents many aspects of this decision were unfortunate, particularly because the prospect of ICT's low-interest loans was one of the few possible sources of money for home improvements available to low-income peoples.

Sewage still flows openly in many parts of the barrio. The sewer project was discontinued due to structural and bureaucratic obstacles. Blueprints for a complete barrio sewer with storm drains existed for years, but because funds kept getting diverted to other projects in the city, Barrio Tulcán became the expendable component. Furthermore, other than the provision of occasional truckloads of crushed-rock ballast, none of the proposed road work has been done. Rather than doing the job twice, the city fathers want to wait until the sewer system is installed before fixing up the streets.

Thus, on the surface at least, the barrio's physical appearance has changed little.

THE PEOPLE—A MACRO-APPROACH

In spite of the absence of significant *visible* change, life for barrio residents has not remained the same. The single greatest thing affecting them over the past three and a half years has been rampant inflation.[1] Between October 1970, the last time that I gathered economic data on a large scale, and July 1974 the cost of living in Colombia rose by 126 per cent (Banco de la República 1974:352). Naturally, those most affected are the poor: barrio residents can vociferously attest to that.

Increasingly, Tulcaneses are losing ground in their struggle to maintain parity with the rising costs. Between 1970 and 1974 the median head of household income rose by 174 Colombian pesos,[2] or an increase of 70 per cent. During the same period the median household income increased by 250 pesos, or 56 per cent. In both cases residents fall far short of keeping up with the cost-of-living rise for the same period. It is important to remember that the poor are less able to absorb this than are most North Americans who have seen dollars shrink in buying power in recent years. Tulcaneses already have their belts about as tight as they can go.

In general, the occupational overview of Tulcaneses still

1. By 1974 the U.S. exchange rate was roughly 25.50 pesos to 1 dollar.

2. The statistical material presented in this chapter comes from interviews administered to a sample of more than 35 per cent of the barrio's household heads (N=101) in July 1974.

can be described as unstable, reflecting a high level of unemployment and underemployment. That is, the majority of workers are never assured of continuous income or work, and when they have jobs they often earn less than minimum wage. These people include small-scale merchants (individuals who run small housefront stores, sell items from carts which they push through Popayán's streets, and repackage and sell herbs and condiments), construction workers (who often work sporadically with days or weeks between jobs), and agriculturalists (who cultivate land in Tulcán and sell produce to their neighbors or work on small farms outside the barrio), as well as residents who wash clothes for a living, work as tailors and seamstresses, and work as maids in the center of town. These categories account for 83.7 per cent of the household heads, an increase of 5.4 per cent from 1970.

The remaining household heads (16.3 per cent in 1974 and 21.7 per cent in 1970) hold jobs in industry, intermediate scale commerce (stores in the center of town), and the municipal or departmental governments. These enterprises are regulated (or at least occasionally spot-checked) by the government, and therefore pay the minimum wage (552 pesos monthly) and provide some social services (medical care, biannual cash bonuses, and retirement funds). But employment in these areas is very limited. Not surprisingly, two-thirds of the jobholders interviewed indicated that they would like to get into another line of work. Three-quarters indicated that they simply wanted more pay.

Although there exists a high level of job turnover and periodic unemployment for many (such as construction workers), the 21 per cent increase in the number of household heads who do not merely regard themselves as between jobs, but actually out of work, is a startling index of the economic situation in the barrio.

In spite of the bleak overall economic picture, some residents appear better off than before. Earlier it was stated that in 1970 the average Standard of Living Score was 7.3. By 1974 this had increased by 15 per cent to an average 8.4. The principal reason for this increase was due to the increment in the number of people now with electricity—up 15 per cent. This reflects the improved electrical service in the barrio; lights (the principal item for which current is used) are more attractive and useful than before. While electricity is responsible in large measure for the rise in Standard of Living Scores, power-line hookups and electrical use itself are in fact very *in*expensive. Thus, capital expenditures for current are not great by barrio standards. The average Standard of Living Score also rose because of a 14 per cent increase in the number of kerosene (and, to a much lesser extent, electric and propane) stoves since 1970. Most of these are small one- or two-burner kerosene stoves which are increasingly used because wood and charcoal are now more difficult to obtain and furthermore are *more* expensive than kerosene. Similarly, the increase in the percentage of indoor toilets and latrines (up 30 per cent) does not represent much of a financial outlay, and the acquisition of one has high priority among residents. A 7 per cent increase in the number of radios reflects a proliferation of inexpensive Japanese, Taiwanese, and Korean radios now available. The only two changes in the average score which cannot be explained easily are increases (although minor in actual number) in record players (8 per cent) and television sets (5 per cent); both of these items represent considerable financial investments and are found only in comparatively well-to-do households. Most people spend little on nonessential items.

THE PEOPLE—A MICRO-APPROACH

Until now I have discussed change in general terms at the barrio level. Included are people who were not living in the area when the initial study was made, but are nevertheless responsible for much of its modification. In order to give a slightly different perspective, I have drawn a comparative sample of thirty household heads, all of whom have lived in Tulcán since 1970.

In general, these "old-timers" have not fared as well as the barrio as a whole. The median rise in head-of-household income is only 54 per cent—16 per cent lower than the barrio in general. The degree of change here is wide and ranges from two instances in which income decreased by 100 per cent to one case (to be discussed shortly) of an individual who increased his earnings by an astronomical 1400 per cent. Significantly though, only seven of the thirty were able to keep pace with inflation by increasing their incomes 126 per cent or

FIGURE 7. Barrio residents relaxing on a Sunday afternoon.

more. On the household level, early residents demonstrated a median increase of 89 per cent, exceeding the general barrio by 33 per cent. At least a third of the households were able to exceed the rate of inflation. Material wealth among these families remained constant, unlike the 15 per cent increase in the Standard of Living Scores by the barrio as a whole.

In the following examples, I will discuss two patterns of familial change found in the barrio. The first is extremely unusual and represents the epitome of economic good fortune desired by so many, but enjoyed by so few. The cyclical nature of the second example is characteristic of what generally is found in Tulcán.

In 1970 Héctor Arias, then a man of twenty-one, lived with his father, mother, teen-age sister, and six-year-old brother in a one-room dirt-floor house. Each morning they went into the hills to cut firewood, which they sold to their neighbors. By supplementing this with the sale of herbs and vegetables which they grew in a large *huerta* (garden), Héctor and his family earned about 200 pesos a month. Most afternoons, after leaving the women to sell the morning's wood, Héctor and his father would walk into town and go their separate ways looking for odd jobs to earn some extra money. Nobody in the family particularly liked the situation and they fondly remembered how, only a few years before, Héctor's father Jaime worked for the municipal government and his mother ran a small stand in the market. A series of unfortunate incidents caused Jaime to lose his job and, after experiencing some bad times, Faustina was forced to leave her job in the market.

Then in September 1971, a friend asked Jaime if he would like to buy his horse and cart. Realizing what a good investment this would be, Jaime sold a piece of land and made the down payment. Héctor became a hauler. Being a hard worker and a very resourceful individual, he became financially successful within a very short time. With the profits the family was able to acquire a market stand for Faustina and she returned to selling vegetables. Within a year they were able to establish Jaime in the business of selling chickens. He now buys day-old Leghorn pullets from an agricultural cooperative in town, spends two and a half months fattening them on Purina chicken feed, and then sells them from his own market stand. Jaime also buys chickens in the market, as well as from his neighbors, for resale, and there is always a supply of eggs which the daughter sells in the barrio. All of this has resulted in tremendous financial gains for the Arias family. Héctor's income has increased by 1400 per cent, and that of the family is up by 1380 per cent since 1970. In 1971 Héctor married and now he and his wife and their two children live in a one-room, dirt-floored, brick and bamboo addition to the main house. His sister Paulina is also married. She and her husband, who contributes 480 pesos per month to the family coffers, and their two children have their own one-room addition in the family compound. Financially life could hardly be better for the Ariases. Their per capita income shows an increase of 576 per cent, the family eats much better, and their material possessions include two new kerosene stoves, one more radio, and a combination radio-turntable.

The Cruz family is much more typical of what the past three years have meant for barrio residents. In 1970 Jorge Cruz and his eldest son were construction workers. When both worked they brought home 1,270 pesos, an earning which put them in the upper three-quarters of barrio household incomes. Although Jorge complained about the unstable nature of his work, he, his wife, and their eight children lived in a comfortable, though cramped, two-room house (with a small kitchen area on the side).

In March 1974, after having worked sporadically for three months, and then been without work for a month, Jorge took one of his teen-age daughters and returned to the rural area where he was born. The coffee harvest was about to begin, and he hoped to earn some money before returning to Popayán. Meanwhile, twenty-year-old José had been drafted and could no longer provide any income for the family. This left eighteen-year-old María and fourteen-year-old Sixto (each making 400 pesos a month) as the breadwinners of the family—to which a new member had been added in 1973. To supplement the family income, Marta, the mother, found a job which paid 180 pesos per month for working eleven hours a day, seven days a week, as a cleaning lady in a clinic. With nine-year-old Nemecio in school, this left six-and-a-half-year-old Patricia in charge of three-year-old Eugenia and sixteen-month-old Francisco. In June, the school where María was employed closed for the summer, leaving her without work.

For almost a month she went jobless, before finding an opening as a secretary which paid 500 pesos a month. At the end of June, Marta quit her job because she felt she could earn more at home taking in wash, which would allow her to be with the children. This proved unsatisfactory and within two weeks she was working again, washing dishes in a restaurant on Popayán's main plaza and earning 600 pesos per month. This was a good job. Because the restaurant is in the center of town and under the eye of municipal authorities (many of whom eat there), the proprietor pays his employees minimum wages and they receive some "social services." Just about this time Sixto lost his job. He had been working as a messenger boy, but the store's owner decided to give Sixto's job to a boy who had worked there before. After spending a few days looking, Sixto found another spot as a messenger boy.

At the end of July four of the family members were working and bringing home a combined total of 1,500 pesos—not much for a family of eight. Furthermore, this income is neither stable nor constant. One month, for example, the family lived off Sixto's 400 pesos. Payments for the family sewing machine must be periodically postponed when the Cruzes have a lean month. The cyclical nature of working and income is the norm for Tulcán's residents.

ATTITUDINAL CHANGE

Change can be gauged in still other ways. In 1970–71 barrio residents possessed a certain esprit de corps: they professed pride in their barrio, although there really was very little community cohesiveness. In 1970 barrio residents rallied around the presidential candidacy of former President General Gustavo Rojas Pinilla. Even though he lost, residents felt that much of his platform aimed at helping the urban poor would be forthcoming. In the early months of 1971, with new national and local administrations, residents were optimistic that they, and others like them, no longer would be the forgotten ones. The discussions that barrio leaders held with local officials, the promises made to them, and the fact that Tulcaneses genuinely wanted these things served to band people together somewhat.

To be sure, there was never any real and meaningful coalescing in the barrio. The idea of living independently and not meddling in the affairs of others was too dominant a life theme. Yet, at another level, barrio identity existed, and residents once talked about Tulcán in proud terms. Often I heard people say how safe and tranquil the barrio was, and how its residents were so much better than the people of surrounding neighborhoods. Now it appears that just the reverse is occurring. No longer are superlatives used in describing the barrio. While residents feel that the barrio "improved" over the past three years (because some of the public utilities are better), they are equally convinced it is a "worse" place to live. Stories of robberies and killings now replace the tales of how in Tulcán one could leave his house unguarded and nothing would be stolen, and how this would be impossible elsewhere in Popayán.

Their changing attitudes are reflected in still other ways. Although residents are still as independent as they were three years ago, they assume a more unified and activist stance in dealing with municipal authorities. For example, in 1973 men working on a muncipal construction site accidentally broke the pipe carrying water into the barrio. Residents were told it would be at least a week before it could be fixed. The following day a couple of hundred Tulcaneses marched into town, armed with placards, and asked to see the director of the waterworks. They then demanded that the broken pipe be repaired. Within three days residents had water. In early August 1974, a similar incident happened, and the problem was handled in much the same way. Proud of their successes, they nevertheless note that people in most other areas of town would not have to demonstrate to get something like that corrected and definitely would not have had to wait even a day for it to be fixed. Residents who used to be content to let the rulers of the Junta de Acción Comunal negotiate with the city fathers, now are seeking direct action themselves, and this seems to be working (cf. Cornelius 1974).

CONCLUSIONS

What can be said in summary about change in Barrio Tulcán? From their perspective, an old axiom is true. Life is changing, but in the process they see everything becoming more expensive and note with chagrin that there is little they can do about it. Lamentably, they point out, they are slipping further behind in their pursuit of the "good life." As they get poorer, they sarcastically and rhetorically ask, who gets richer? The answer, they say, is the rich. This feeling produces further disenchantment with a system which they are convinced is an exploitative one designed to hold them down. Their seeming inability to really rectify the situation or have it corrected is frustrating and will increasingly result in protestations of one type or another. This appears to produce tangible results. Perhaps when they recognize the potentially beneficial aspects of this strategy, promises will indeed be kept, their situation will improve, and once again they will view life with a degree of guarded optimism.

References

Aragón, Arcesio
1930. *Popayán*. Popayán: Imprenta y Encuadernación del Departamento del Cauca.
Banco de la República
1974. Indice de precios al mayor del comercio en general. *Revista del Banco de la República* 47 (556):352.
Banton, Michael
1957. *West African city: a study of tribal life in Freetown*. London: Oxford University Press.
Butterworth, Douglas S.
1962. A study of the urbanization process among Mixtec migrants from Tilantongo in Mexico City. *América Indígena* 22:257–74.
Camacho de Pinto, Teresa
1970. *Colombia: el proceso de urbanización y sus factores relacionados*. Tunja: Universidad Pedagogica y Tecnologica de Colombia, Ediciones "La Rana y el Águila."
Cardona Gutíerrez, Ramiro
1968. Migración, urbanización y marginalidad. In *Urbanización y marginalidad*, pp. 63–87. Seminario nacional sobre urbanización y marginalidad, marzo 28–31, 1968. Bogotá: Asociación Colombiana de Facultades de Medicina, División de Estudios de Población.
Castrillon Arboleda, Diego
1970. *De la colonia al subdesarrollo*. Popayán: Editorial Universidad.
Centro de Estudios sobre Desarrollo Económico (CEDE)
1968. *Empleo y desempleo en Colombia*. Bogotá, D.E.: Ediciones Universidad de Los Andes.

134   References

Chance, John K.
1971. Kinship and urban residence: household and family organization in a suburb of Oaxaca, Mexico. *Journal of the Steward Anthropological Society* 2(2):122–47.

Cornelius, Wayne A.
1974. Urbanization and political demand-making: political participation among the migrant poor in Latin American cities. *American Political Science Review* 68 (3):1125–46.

Cornelius, Wayne, and Felicity Trueblood, eds.
1974. *Latin American urban research*, vol. 4, *Anthropological perspectives on Latin American urbanization*. Beverly Hills, Calif.: Sage Publications.

Crist, Raymond E.
1950. The personality of Popayán. *Rural Sociology* 15:130–40.
1971. Popayán revisited. *Américas* 23(4):25–32.

Currier, Richard L.
1966. The hot-cold syndrome and symbolic balance in Mexican and Spanish-American medicine. *Ethnology* 9:251–64.

Davis, Allison; Burleigh B. Gardner; and Mary R. Gardner
1941. *Deep south*. Chicago: University of Chicago Press.

Denitch, Bette S.
1969. Social mobility and industrialization in a Yugoslav town. Ph.D. dissertation, University of California, Berkeley.

Departamento Administrativo Nacional de Estadística (DANE)
1967. *XIII censo nacional de población, resumen general*. Bogotá, D.E.: Imprenta Nacional.

Departamento Nacional de Planeación (DNP)
1969. *La población en Colombia: realidad, perspectivas, y política*. Bogotá, D.E.: Imprenta Nacional.

Dix, Robert
1967. *Colombia: the political dimensions of change*. New Haven: Yale University Press.

Epstein, A. L.
1957. African townsmen. *Rhodes-Livingstone Journal* 22:67–70.
1958. *Politics in an urban African community*. Manchester, England: Manchester University Press.
1967. Urbanization and social change in Africa. *Current Anthropology* 8:275–98.

Epstein, David G.
1973. *Brasília, plan and reality: a study of planned and spontaneous urban development*. Berkeley: University of California Press.

Fals Borda, Orlando
1969. *Subversion and social change in Colombia*. New York: Columbia University Press.

Feindt, Waltraut, and Harley L. Browning
1970. Return migration: its significance in an industrial metropolis and an agricultural town in Mexico. Paper prepared for the Latin American Regional Population Conference, Mexico City, August 17–22, 1970.

Flinn, William L.
1966. Rural to urban migration: a Colombian case. Research paper 19:1–42. Land Tenure Center, University of Wisconsin, Madison.

Foster, George M.
1965. Peasant society and the image of limited good. *American Anthropologist* 67:292–315.

1967. *Tzintzuntzan: Mexican peasants in a changing world.* Boston: Little, Brown.
1971. A second look at limited good. Paper prepared for the Seventieth Annual Meeting of the American Anthropological Association, New York, November 18–21, 1971.
Foster, George M., and Robert V. Kemper, eds.
1974. *Anthropologists in cities.* Boston: Little, Brown.
Fried, Jacob
1959. Acculturation and mental health among Indian migrants in Peru. In *Culture and Mental Health,* ed. M. K. Opler. New York: Macmillan.
Friedl, John, and Noel J. Chrisman, eds.
1975. *City ways: a selective reader in urban anthropology.* New York: Crowell.
Germani, Gino
1961. Inquiry into the social effects of urbanization in a working-class sector of Greater Buenos Aires. In *Urbanization in Latin America,* ed. Philip M. Hauser, pp. 206–33. New York: International Documents Service.
Gillin, John
1947. *Moche: a Peruvian coastal community.* Institute of Social Anthropology publication 3. Washington: Smithsonian Institution.
González, Nancie L.
1974. *The city of gentlemen: Santiago de Los Caballeros.* In *Anthropologists in cities,* ed. G. M. Foster and R. V. Kemper, pp. 19–40. Boston: Little, Brown.
Gutkind, Peter C. W.
1960. Congestion and overcrowding: an African urban problem. *Human Organization* 19:129–34.
1961. Urban conditions in Africa. *Town Planning Review* 32:20–32.
Guzmán Campos, G.; O. Fals Borda; and E. Umaña Luna
1962. *La violencia en Colombia.* Bogotá, D.E.: Ediciones Tercer Mundo.
Hammel, Eugene
1969. *Power in Ica: the structural history of a Peruvian community.* Boston: Little, Brown.
Havens, A. Eugene, and William L. Flinn
1970a. The power structure in a shantytown. In *Internal colonialism and structural change in Colombia,* ed. A. E. Havens and W. L. Flinn, pp. 93–107. New York: Praeger.
1970b. Urban lower class voter participation and political attitudes. In *Internal colonialism and structural change in Colombia,* ed. A. E. Havens and W. L. Flinn, pp. 108–27. New York: Praeger.
Herrick, Bruce H.
1965. *Urban migration and economic development in Chile.* Cambridge, Mass.: M.I.T. Press.
Hirschman, A. O.
1963. *Journeys toward progress: studies of economic policy-making in Latin America.* New York: The Twentieth Century Fund.
Hobsbawm, Eric J.
1963. The revolutionary situation in Colombia. *World Today* 19:248–58.
Ingham, John M.
1970. On Mexican folk medicine. *American Anthropologist* 72(1):76–87.
Instituto de Crédito Territorial (ICT)
1970. *Estudio físico del barrio* [Tulcán] *en Popayán.* Popayán: Oficina de Planeación, Sección de Investigaciones y Estadística.

Kelly, Isabel
  1961. Mexican spiritualism. Kroeber Anthropological Society Papers
        25:191–206.
Kemper, Robert V.
  1970. The anthropological study of migrants to Latin American cities.
        Kroeber Anthropological Society Papers 42:1–25.
  1971. Migration and adaptation of Tzintzuntzan peasants in Mexico City.
        Ph.D. dissertation, University of California, Berkeley.
  1974. Tzintzuntzeños in Mexico City: the anthropologist among peasant
        migrants. In Anthropologists in cities, ed. G. M. Foster and R. V.
        Kemper, pp. 63–91. Boston: Little, Brown.
Leeds, Anthony, and Elizabeth Leeds
  1970. Brazil and the myth of urban rurality: urban experiences, work, and
        values in "squatments" of Rio de Janiero and Lima. In City and
        country in the Third World, ed. A. J. Field, pp. 229–85. Cambridge,
        Mass.: Schenkman.
Lewis, Oscar
  1952. Urbanization without breakdown: a case study. Scientific Monthly
        75:31–41.
  1959. The culture of the vecindad in Mexico City: two case studies. Actas
        del 33 Congreso Internacional de Americanistas, 1:386–402. San José,
        Costa Rica: Lehman.
  1969. Possessions of the poor. Scientific American 221(4):114–24.
  1970. La cultura material de los pobres. América Indígena 30(4):945–91.
Lipman, Aaron, and A. Eugene Havens
  1965. The Colombian violencia: an ex post facto experiment. Social Forces
        44(2):238–45.
McGreevey, William P.
  1968. Causas de la migración interna en Colombia. In Empleo y desem-
        pleo en Colombia, pp. 211–21. Centro de Estudios sobre Desarrollo
        Económico (CEDE). Bogotá, D.E.: Ediciones Universidad de Los
        Andes.
Mangin, William P.
  1960. Mental health and migration to the cities: a Peruvian case. Annals of
        the New York Academy of Sciences 84:911–17.
  1967a. Latin American squatter settlements: a problem and a solution.
        Latin American Research Review 2(3):65–98.
  1967b. Squatter settlements. Scientific American 217(4):21–29.
Mangin, William P., and Jerome Cohen
  1964. Cultural and psychological characteristics of mountain migrants to
        Lima, Peru. Sociologus 14:81–88.
Martínez Delgado, Luis
  1959. Popayán, ciudad procera. Bogotá: Editorial Kelly.
Matos Mar, José
  1961. Migration and urbanization—the "Barriadas" of Lima: an example of
        integration into urban life. In Urbanization in Latin America, ed.
        Philip M. Hauser, pp. 280–93. New York: International Documents
        Service.
Mayer, Philip
  1961. Townsmen or tribesmen: conservatism and the process of urbaniza-
        tion in a South African city. London: Oxford University Press.
  1962. Migrancy and the study of Africans in towns. American Anthro-
        pologist 64(3):576–91.

Mitchell, J. Clyde
    1951. A note on the urbanization of Africans on the copperbelt. *Rhodes-Livingstone Journal* 12:20–27.
    1956. Urbanization, detribalization and stabilization in southern Africa: a problem of definition and measurement. In *Social implications of industrialization and urbanization in Africa south of the Sahara*, pp. 693–710. Paris: UNESCO.
    1960. The anthropological study of urban communities. *African Studies* 19:169–72.
    1966. Theoretical orientations in African urban studies. In *The social anthropology of complex societies*, ed. Michael Banton, pp. 37–68. ASA Monograph, no. 4. London: Tavistock.
    1969. The concept and use of social networks. In *Social networks in urban situations*, ed. J. C. Mitchell, pp. 1–50. Manchester, England: University of Manchester Press.
Murray, Henry A.
    1943. *Thematic apperception test manual*. Cambridge, Mass.: Harvard University Press.
Orellana S., Carlos L.
    1973. Mixtec migrants in Mexico City: a case study of urbanization. *Human Organization* 32(3):273–83.
Peattie, Lisa Redfield
    1968. *The view from the barrio*. Ann Arbor: University of Michigan Press.
Pineda, Roberto
    1960. *El impacto de la violencia en el Tolima: el caso de el Líbano*. Monografías Sociológicas, no. 6. Bogotá: Universidad Nacional de Colombia.
Pi-Sunyer, Oriol
    1973. *Zamora: change and continuity in a Mexican town*. New York: Holt, Rinehart and Winston.
Press, Irwin
    1969. Urban illness: physicians, curers and dual use in Bogotá. *Journal of Health and Social Behavior* 10(3):209–18.
    1971. The urban curandero. *American Anthropologist* 73(3):741–56.
Price, John
    1973. *Tijuana: urbanization in a border culture*. Notre Dame, Ind.: University of Notre Dame Press.
Ravicz, Robert
    1967. Compadrinazgo. In *Handbook of Middle American Indians*, ed. R. Wauchope and M. Nash, 6:238–52. Austin: University of Texas Press.
Reina, Ruben E.
    1973. *Paraná: social boundaries in an Argentine city*. Austin: University of Texas Press.
Rico Castillo, Ana, and Jorge Antonio Rey
    1969. *Estudio sociológico de la población artesanal de Popayán*. Instituto de Crédito Territorial. Bogotá, D.E.: Oficina de Planeación, Sección de Investigaciones y Estadística.
Roberts, Bryan R.
    1970. The social organization of low-income families. In *Masses in Latin America*, ed. I. L. Horowitz, pp. 345–82. New York: Oxford University Press.
    1973. *Organizing strangers: poor families in Guatemala City*. Austin: University of Texas Press.

Rogers, Everett M.
  1969. *Modernization among peasants: the impact of communication.* New York: Holt, Rinehart and Winston.
Rollwagen, Jack R.
  1972. A comparative framework for the investigation of the city-as-context: a discussion of the Mexican case. *Urban Anthropology* 1(1):68–86.
Safa, Helen Icken
  1974. *The urban poor of Puerto Rico: a study in development and inequality.* New York: Holt, Rinehart and Winston.
Sayres, William C.
  1956. Ritual kinship and negative affect. *American Sociological Review* 2:348–52.
Service, Elman R., and Helen S. Service
  1965. General remarks on rural Paraguay. In *Contemporary cultures and societies of Latin America,* ed. D. B. Heath and R. N. Adams, pp. 70–84. New York: Random House.
Southall, Aidan, ed.
  1973. *Urban anthropology: cross-cultural studies of urbanization.* New York: Oxford University Press.
Szulc, Tad
  1959. *Twilight of the tyrants.* New York: Henry Holt.
Urrutia, Miguel
  1968. Métodos para medir los diferentes tipos de subempleo y de desempleo en Colombia. In *Empleo y desempleo en Colombia,* pp. 23–38. Centro de Estudios sobre Desarrollo Económico (CEDE). Bogotá, D.E.: Ediciones Universidad de Los Andes.
Uzzell, Douglas, and Ronald Provencher
  1976. *Urban anthropology.* Dubuque, Iowa: William C. Brown.
Ward, Barbara
  1960. Cash or credit crops? an examination of some implications of peasant commercial production with special reference to the multiplicity of traders and middlemen. *Economic Development and Cultural Change* 8(2):148–63.
Warner, W. Lloyd, and Paul S. Lunt
  1941. *The social life of a modern community.* New Haven: Yale University Press.
  1942. *The status system of a modern community.* New Haven: Yale University Press.
  1945. *The social systems of American ethnic groups.* New Haven: Yale University Press.
Warner, W. Lloyd, et al.
  1949. *Democracy in Jonesville.* New York: Harper.
Weaver, Thomas, and Douglas White, eds.
  1972. *The anthropology of urban environments.* SAA Monograph Series, no. 11. Boulder: Society for Applied Anthropology.
Whiteford, Andrew H.
  1954a. Holy Week in Popayán. *Américas* 6(4):6–8, 42–43.
  1954b. Semana Santa en Popayán. *Imagenes* 10:10–12.
  1956. Popayán Christmas. *Américas* 8(12):7–10.
  1960. *Two cities in Latin America: a comparative description of social classes.* Beloit, Wisconsin: Logan Museum of Anthropology.
  1963. Social change in Popayán. In *Land reform and social change in Colombia.* Land Tenure Center, Discussion Paper 4:12–17. Madison: University of Wisconsin Press.

1970. Aristocracy, oligarchy, and cultural change in Colombia. In *City and country in the Third World*, ed. Arthur J. Field, pp. 63–91. Cambridge, Mass.: Schenkman.

1976. *A traditional Andean city: Popayán at mid-century*. East Lansing: Latin American Studies Center, Michigan State University.

Whiteford, Michael B.

1974a. Barrio Tulcán: fieldwork in a Colombian city. In *Anthropologists in cities*, ed. G. M. Foster and R. V. Kemper, pp. 41–62. Boston: Little, Brown.

1974b. Neighbors at a distance: social relations in a low-income Colombian barrio. In *Latin American urban research*, vol. 4, *Anthropological perspectives on Latin American urbanization*, ed. W. A. Cornelius and F. M. Trueblood, pp. 157–81. Beverly Hills, Calif.: Sage Publications.

1976. Avoiding obscuring generalizations: differences in migrants and their adaptations to an urban environment. In *New approaches to the study of migrations*, ed. J. D. Uzzell and D. Guillet. Houston: Rice University.

Whitten, Jr., Norman E.

1969. Strategies of adaptive mobility in the Colombian-Equadorian littoral. *American Anthropologist* 71(2):228–42.

Wirth, Louis

1938. Urbanism as a way of life. *American Journal of Sociology* 44:1–24.

Wolf, Eric R.

1966. Kinship, friendship, and patron-client relations in complex societies. In *The social anthropology of complex societies*, ed. Michael Banton, pp. 1–22. ASA Monograph 4. London: Tavistock.

1976. Avoiding obscuring generalizations: differences in migrants and their adaptations to an urban environment. In *Anthropologists on migration: theoretical issues reconsidered*, ed. J. D. Uzzell and D. Guillet. Houston: Rice University.

Index

141